101 TORCHON PATTERNS

with coloured technical diagrams

101 TORCHON PATTERNS

with coloured technical diagrams

Robin Lewis-Wild

B. T. Batsford Ltd · London

Acknowledgment

My gratitude to my friends and family for their help, support and advice which made this possible. A special thanks to my lace instructors, my students, and my lace friends; their enthusiasm and dedication have been the inspiration for this book. I would like to thank especially the following:

Suzanne Van Ruymbeke-Deraedt – my most recent lace instructor and initial consultant on materials for this publication, an inspiration and unequalled source of knowledge, information and materials.

Mme Maria (and Jean) Cools – also a recent instructor who aside from her encouragement and knowledge, has given gifts of lace which have been shared by all who visit and whose work and patterns have been shared willingly with me and other dedicated lacemakers.

Wendell Adams – the photographer of the lace and friend.

W.A. Crouch – friend and consultant.

Dedication

This book is dedicated to Kenneth Atkins, without whom it would not have seen completion.

ISBN 0 7134 7294 4

Typeset by Tek Art Ltd, Kent
and printed in Hong Kong by
Colorcraft Ltd, Hong Kong
for the publishers
B.T. Batsford Ltd
583 Fulham Road
London SW6 5BY

Distributed in the United States
of America exclusively by:
Robin's Bobbins
and other things
215 Murphy Lane
Mineral Bluff, GA 30559-2906

CONTENTS

INTRODUCTION

The purpose of this work is to offer a wide selection of patterns for intermediate students so that they have an opportunity to build skills and practice techniques beyond basic lesson-work before continuing into more advanced work or other areas of lace. Heretofore there have been few sources of patternwork at this level. There are already numerous books on a more advanced level of Torchon and in other families of lace. Intermediate students, or those just completing basic lessonwork, have often been discouraged as they have not acquired the skills and understanding enough to execute work at this level. Nor have they progressed to a level that they should leave the area of Torchon and start with just basic understanding and skills to new areas of Honiton, Bucks Point, Flanders and so on without further instruction. It is hoped instructors will find this material useful to guide their students eager for and needing more lessonwork in Torchon.

About the patterns

The patterns include antique patterns, modified traditional patterns, patterns from antique clothing and the author's own designs, similarity of these to any existing patterns is merely coincidental. They have been divided into five basic categories: edgings, insertions, corners, bookmarks and medallions. Each pattern has a pricking on graph, a photo of the lacework, and a coloured technical diagram. Numerous skills have been built into the material, in the way of various motifs, spiders, tallies, fans, footings and so on. There is a listing at the top of each pattern describing the particular techniques covered in each. They have been arranged according to the number of bobbins, some requiring considerably less than others, but not necessarily at a less advanced level. Each pattern gives the number of bobbins used, and the placement of each is given for the diagram (horizontally across the pattern at a given point). A separate starting point is given to the pricking (usually following the diagonal and along the beginning of a motif), selected placement on the pattern to begin a completed project of lace – as for a handkerchief, for

instance. There is no one 'right' choice for this beginning, but one must consider finding an area that sewings will be least noticeable when the piece is completed – if possible along a cloth stitch area is a good choice. The small completed projects are included to offer encouragement and incentive to the student as he or she gains a sense of achievement upon completion of a project not overwhelming in time.

In addition to giving the starting point (often difficult for the student), the patterns have been arranged, wherever possible, to fall toward the outside edges of the pages, making copying (for personal use only) easy. If this method is desired, the photocopy should then be placed on a dark, quality parchment (rubbing paraffin over the upper surface will make pricking easier) and the pattern pricked for a suitable working surface. The graph has been left beneath the pricked patterns to make transcribing them to a larger or finer grid possible, and to retain the accuracy of the pricking. Each pricking is aligned on the graph starting from an inch mark on the top and the left side to make measuring easier.

Some lacemakers are accustomed to working the footing to the left, and some the right, depending upon the tradition of the lace or that of their teacher. This difference, along with the path of the worker travelling from left to right, or right to left, between two pins on a given level (see Motifs on page ix) seems always a bone of contention. Here the choice has been made to place the straight edge of the pattern on the left, as it is taught in Belgium. For those who choose not to work with their patterns in this direction, they may copy and flop or reverse their pattern or working direction. There are some motifs in which a combination of directions sometimes is used, making the right side a mirrored image of the left (in a triangle, see pages 54 and 55 for instance), but even here the opposite direction for each side can be used. In order not to confuse the student, consistency has been used in the direction of the work. However, it is important that the student understands these differences, and that he or she be able to work in either direction. There is no right or wrong method, although a lace should be made true according to its place of origin (for instance Bucks Point with edging on the right, Tonder and Lille with footing on the left).

Ratio of thread to the size of the graph

The prickings have been made on graph-paper size ten squares to the inch throughout the text. Size 80/2 linen has been used and 20/2 for gimp in order to make the stitches more distinguishable. The worker can transpose the patterns to eight squares to the inch graph paper and use sizes 40/2-60/2 linen. Sizes 60/2-80/2 linen can be used on the ten squares to the inch prickings. When metric graph paper is used 100/2-120/2 size linen thread is advised. Linen is always preferred to cotton when the sizes are available.

Diagram and photo

Diagram and photo are shown together to make reference easy. The photos, made to actual size, have been taken of the working side of the lace to assist in the working of the pattern and to eliminate confusion. Once the student understands the method of colour diagramming, it will be possible to continue work on one's own.

Using the pricking and diagram

Small x's at the beginning of prickings indicate passive pairs that do not begin at specific pinholes but which are hung over temporary pins to start the work. These pins are removed soon after the work is begun, and the threads pulled carefully down into place.

There are two ways of starting:

1 On the pricking, a method is suggested which may end with sewings. Start along the diagonal indicated and find the matching point on the diagram.

2 The diagram indicates the pairs hung on horizontally. Start as suggested and find the corresponding point within the pricking.

Do not try to start at the top of the pricking and at the top of the diagram. They will not always correlate.

Equipment

As far as equipment is concerned, a Belgium-style lace pillow approximately 18in in diameter is the most versatile. Strips of lace, cornered work, bookmarks and medallions, all can be worked on this round, flat pillow. If one intends only   make lengths of straight lace, a pillow with a bolster would suit better. Cornered work is executed by completing one side and one corner and then moving the lace up on the pattern. This is done by releasing all weight off of the working threads and bobbins, unpinning the lacework, and sliding the work back to fit over a repeat or two of the pattern. Pins are then replaced and work continues. There are two methods to this: one is using a cover cloth beneath the bobbins and threads, making an envelope up over the bobbins and pinning both sides – lifting the weight off and pinning the cloth to the pillow while removing pins. The other method is to lengthen the working threads, and separate them into two or more groups, making a slip-knot out of each batch of threads through which a pin is placed further up on the pillow, taking the weight off the threads and bobbins. This latter method seems the best for travelling with a working pillow to avoid disarray and broken threads.

Some prefer a longer pin or a sturdier one, but 26mm x 0.53mm should be adequate for most work. A pin cushion is a necessity so that one does not become accustomed to using the pillow, wearing a spot through the cover prematurely. Also the pins get in the way of working the lace, especially on corners and medallions. This can become a bad habit, best to avoid from the beginning. A no. 15 crochet hook is suggested for sewings.

1.COLOUR KEY TO COLOUR DIAGRAMMING

The colour diagrams are in accordance with the international colour coding, with the exception of the colours yellow and blue which have been replaced by black. There is, therefore, a notation discerning these differences. This method of diagramming has been widely used for its reliable indication of the stitchwork, making working the lace, discussion and correspondence easy, regardless of language, once the worker becomes familiar with the technique.

—— **Red** represents stitches worked in *Whole Stitch (cross twist, cross twist)*. When necessary *Whole Stitch* will be abbreviated WS

—— **Green** represents stitches worked in *Half Stitch (cross twist)*. When necessary *half stitch* will be abbreviated HS.

—— **Purple** represents stitches worked in *Cloth Stitch (cross, twist, cross)*. When necessary *Cloth Stitch* will be abbreviated CS.
cloth stitch is also called *linen* or *linen stitch*.

=== **Black** is used instead of yellow normally used for single thread reference. These include:

—— **Gimp**–A single thick black line represents single and double gimp as indicated.

▤ **Tally**–Two pairs are used as single threads to weave the dense square. (See p.5)

❀ **Leaf**–Two pairs are used as single threads to weave the leaf.

❁ **Daisy**–Four or more leaves combine to make the flower or daisy with the pairs crossing in the centre in Cloth Stitch (see Daisies or flowers p. xi), or as braids (see Braids or plaits p. xi). Most often there are six or eight leaves in the daisies.
(The tallies, leaves and daisies are also referred to as leadwork when used as fillings in Honiton, and as Les pointes d'espirit by the French.)

=== **Braid** or **Plait**–A thin double black line is used instead of blue to represent two pairs woven as plaits or braids.

Note: A dash in red indicates an additional twist

Stitches

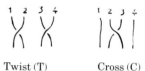

Twist (T)   Cross (C)

Special Note:

There is a difference in the naming of the stitches between countries. The stitches and subsequent diagramming for this text have been done according to the Belgian method. To avoid confusion special attention should be given to the stitch and ground diagrams which follow.

A–Whole stitch (CTCT) (referred to as Cloth Stitch and twist or Whole Stitch and twist in the UK)
(red)

B–Cloth Stitch (CTC) or Linen Stitch (referred to as Whole stitch in the UK)
(purple)

C–Half Stitch (CT)
(green)

Grounds

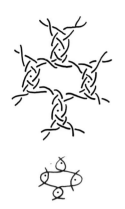

A–Whole stitch

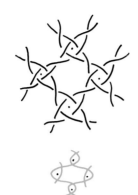

B–Torchon

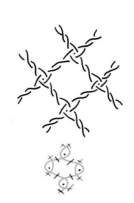

C–Dieppe

D–Half stitch

N.B.   See Rosepoint, p. x for examples of more complex grounds

Geometric motifs

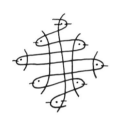

A1–Cloth stitch
diamond

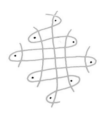

A2–Half stitch
diamond

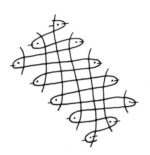

B1–Cloth stitch
rectangle

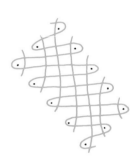

B2–Half stitch
rectangle

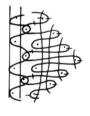

C1–Cloth stitch
triangle

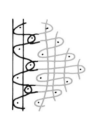

C2–Half stitch
triangle

D1–Cloth stitch
chevron/heart

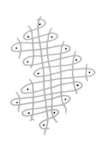

D2–Half stitch
chevron/heart

E1–Cloth stitch
trail

E2–Half stitch
trail

F1–Cloth stitch
window

F2–Half stitch
window

Rosepoint

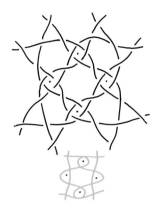

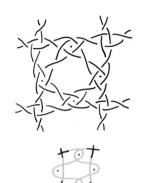

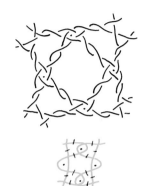

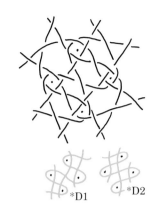

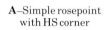

| **A**–Simple rosepoint with HS corner | **B**–Rosepoint with WS corners | **C**–Rosepoint in Dieppe stitch | ***D**–Diagonal Rosepoint (in Half Stitch) |

Order of working the pin holes

| **A**–#1,#2,#3,#4 *or* #1,#3,#2,#4 | **B**–#1,#2,#3,#4 *or* #1,#3,#2,#4 | **C**–#1,#2,#3,#4 *or* #1,#3,#2,#4 | ***D1**–#1,#2,HS,#3,#4 ***D2**–#1,#3,HS,#2,#4 |

*****D1**–*This order of working the diagonal rosepoint creates a diagonal design to the left.*
*****D2**–*This order of working the diagonal rosepoint creates a diagonal design to the right.*

Spiders

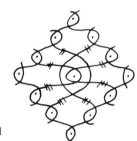

A–Small

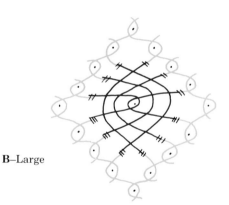

B–Large

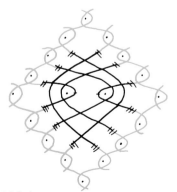

C–Spider with hole

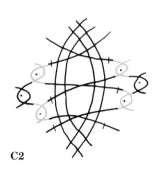

C2

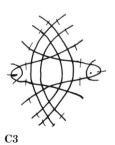

C3

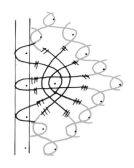
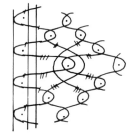
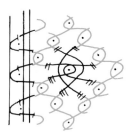
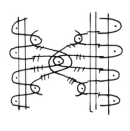

| D1 | D2 | D3 | D4 |

D–Spider using sewing edge

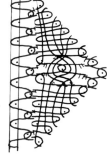
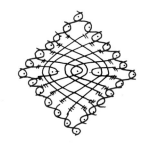

E–Compound spider   **F**–Spider in cloth   **G**–Double spider

Tally *(See Detail, p.5)*

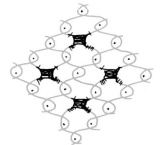

A–Single tally in ground   **B**–Single tally on the diagonal   **C**–4 tallies with ground   **D**–4 tallies compound

Daisies or flowers

Leaves crossed at centre in Cloth Stitch.
Leaves crossed at centre with BRAID/PLAIT CROSSING (*See* Braids).

A–4 point flower
Crossing 4 pairs   **B**–6 point flower
Crossing 6 pairs   **C**–8 point flower
Crossing 8 pairs   **D**–10 point flower
Crossing 10 pairs

Braids or plaits

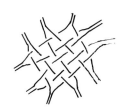

A–Single braid or plait   **B**–Crossing 2 braids
(4 pairs)   **C**–Crossing 3 braids
(6 pairs)   **D**–Crossing 4 braids
(8 pairs)   **E**–Crossing 5 braids
(10 pairs)

xi

Gimp

One thick black line indicates a single gimp or 1 pair as indicated. A single gimp is referred to as 1G, one pair as 1PG, two single gimps as 2G, and two pairs as 2PG.

A–Passing 1 gimp with 3 twists

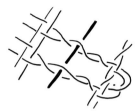

B–Passing gimp without twists

C–Passing 2PG or 2G in cloth stitch

D–Passing 2PG or 2G separated with twists

E–Passing 2PG or 2G together with twists

F–Crossing 2PG

Fans

A–Cloth Stitch with twist on edge

B–Cloth Stitch with WS on outer edge

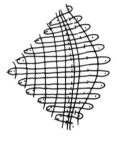
B1–Cloth Stitch with WS and additional twist on worker

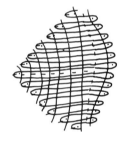
B2–Cloth Stitch with WS and additional twists on passives

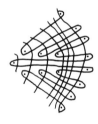
C–Trellis in WS

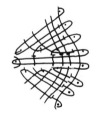
C1–Trellis with CS exchanging worker

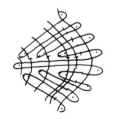
C2–Trellis with CS using 1 worker

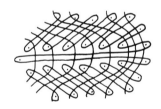
C3–Elongated trellis

D–Gimp as Cloth Stitch Fan

D1–Gimp as trellis fan

D2–Gimp on edge of trellis with CS

D3–Gimp on edge of trellis with CS

Picot

A1–Simple on right
Do not use

A2–Simple on left
Do not use

B1–Single knotted picot on right – *used with braid*

B2–Single knotted picot on left – *used with braid*

C1–Double picot to the right – *used most often in Flanders, Paris, Binche, etc.*

C2–Double picot to the left – *used most often in Bucks Point.*

Footing or sewing edge

Interchangeable terms. Here *footing* will be used to denote sewing side of an edging which has a footing and head (fan side), and *sewing edge* will be used to refer to the edges of insertions.

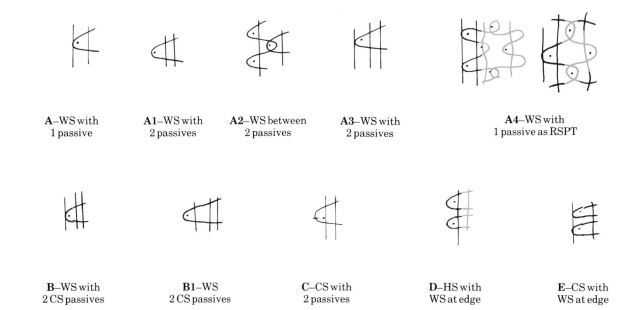

A–WS with
1 passive

A1–WS with
2 passives

A2–WS between
2 passives

A3–WS with
2 passives

A4–WS with
1 passive as RSPT

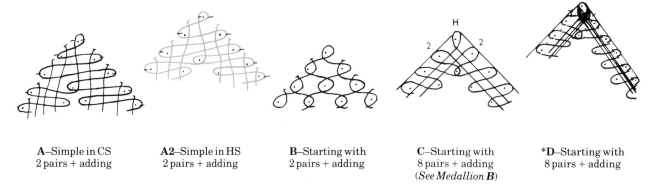

B–WS with
2 CS passives

B1–WS
2 CS passives

C–CS with
2 passives

D–HS with
WS at edge

E–CS with
WS at edge

Techniques

Starts

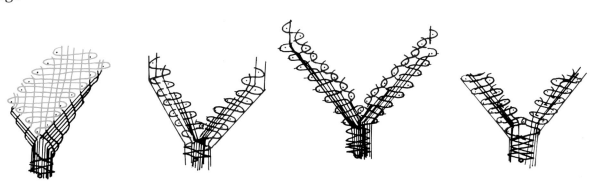

A–Simple in CS
2 pairs + adding

A2–Simple in HS
2 pairs + adding

B–Starting with
2 pairs + adding

C–Starting with
8 pairs + adding
(*See Medallion B*)

***D**–Starting with
8 pairs + adding

*D To begin with whole stitch start with 6 pairs

Endings

A–With pairs outside
Exchanging worker

B–With pairs inside
WS sewing edge, **A**
*Exchanging workers
with outside pair*

C–With pairs inside
WS sewing edge, **A1**
*Exchanging worker
with inside pairs*

D–Eliminating pairs
Single worker per side

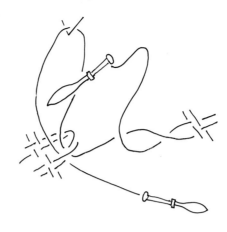

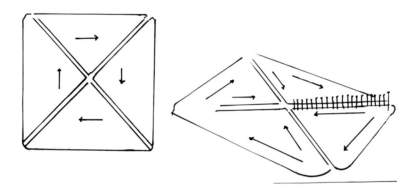

Medallion or mat

A Method of working in triangular sections (*making 4 corners*) starting along the diagonal from the outside adding pairs from the outside to the inside. The finish is also made along the same diagonal as the starting line, taking each pair out at its appropriate pin hole with an individual sewing.

Note: Make all sewings before all bobbins and threads are removed.

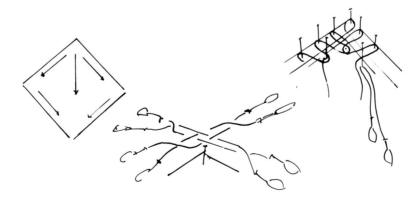

B Method of working beginning at the top adding pairs until the outermost corners are reached, then pairs begin to be eliminated individually along both sides until the lower three holes are reached. The final pairs are eliminated like the top holes were begun, taking two out on each side and four at the last pin hole. (*See* Medallions, on pages 122-127.)

2. COLOUR KEY EXAMPLES OF USE

Colour Key (Example 1)
25 pairs
(pricking on p. xviii)

Ground–WS, **A**
Motif–CS chevron, **D1**
Spider–Small, **A**
Sewing edge–WS, **A**

The worker is encouraged to interchange stitches wherever possible to alter the existing pattern in order to create his or her own version of the pattern. It is important, however, to keep in mind that the major factor in designing lace is the contrast between the design (toilé) and the ground (reseau). Note the example below fails to achieve a pleasing contrast between the floral design and the background.

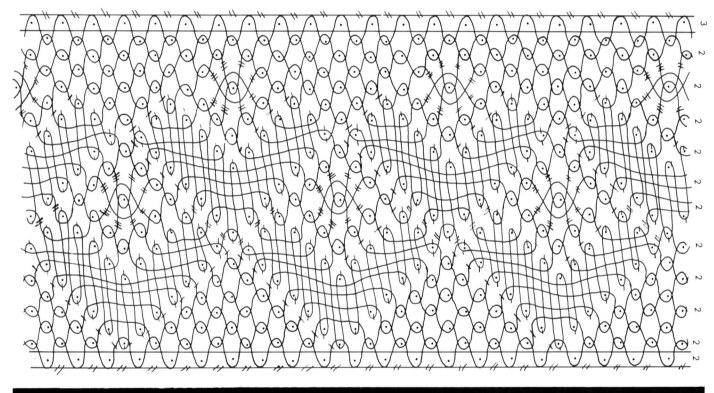

Colour Key (Example 2)
25 pairs
(pricking on p. xviii)

Ground–Torchon, **B**
Motif–CS diamond, **A1**/HS chevron, **D2**
Sewing edge–WS, **A**

In example two, the contrast between the motifs and background is more successful. The design is easier to identify. The difference in density of the Cloth Stitch diamonds and the Half Stitch chevrons works well, and both are easily distinguished from the Torchon ground. This simple exercise merely demonstrates the use of the colour diagramming and emphasizes the necessary discretion needed in the selection of alternate stitches.

Example 1 – Pricking
25 pairs
(*diagram and photo p. xvi*)

Example 2 – Pricking
25 pairs
(*diagram and photo p. xvii*)

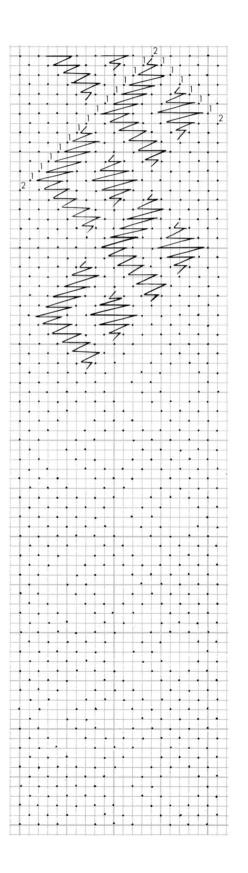

3.EDGINGS

Edging–1
5 pairs + 4 pairs gimps

Ground–Torchon, **B**
Gimp–Passing 2PG, **C** or **D** and crossing 2PG, **F**
Spider–With hole, **C3**
Footing–CS with 2CS passives, **C**

Detail
Gimp spider with hole, **C3**

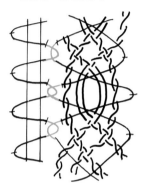

DETAIL   EDGING 1.

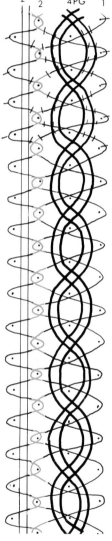

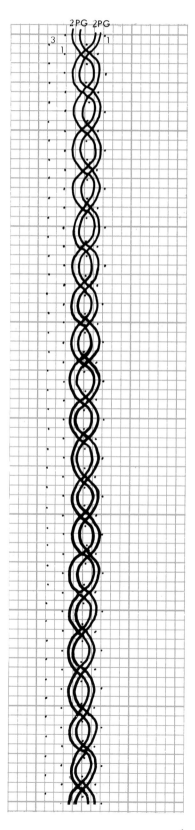

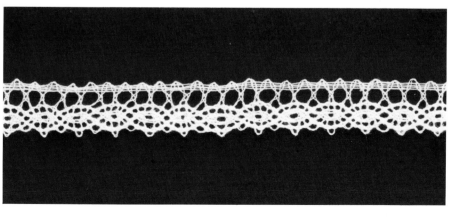

Edging–2 and Edging–3
8 pairs   9 pairs

Ground–(2) Dieppe, **C** and (3) WS, **A**
Fan–(2) and (3) (*one pin hole*) CS with WS, **B**
Footing–(2) WS, **A** and (3) WS with 2 CS
    passives, **B**

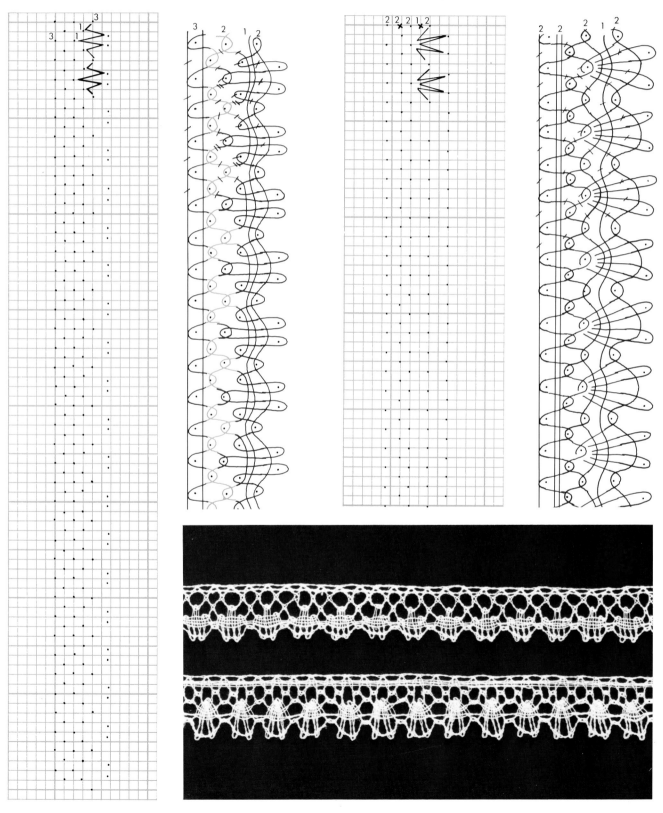

Edging–4A and 4B
11 pairs

Ground–(4A) Dieppe, **C** and (4B) WS, **A**
Fan–(4A) Trellis with Cloth Stitch, **C1**, (4B) **C2**
Footing–(4A and 4B) WS with 2 CS passives, **B**

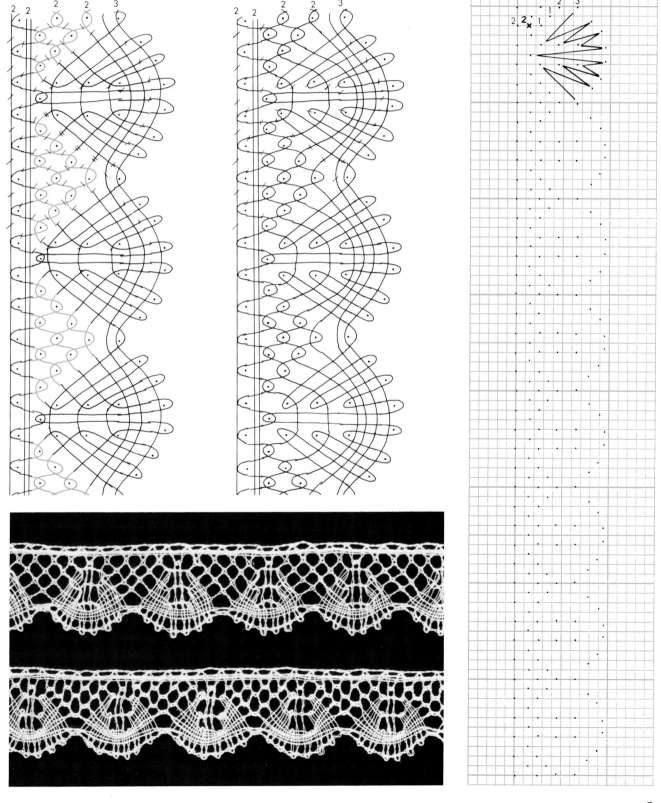

Edging–5
13 pairs

Stitch–CS, **B**
Braid–Crossing 4 pairs/2 braids, **B**
Picot–Single knotted, **B1**
Fan–Trellis with CS (variation), **C2** or, **D2** (without gimp)
   Footing–WS, **A**

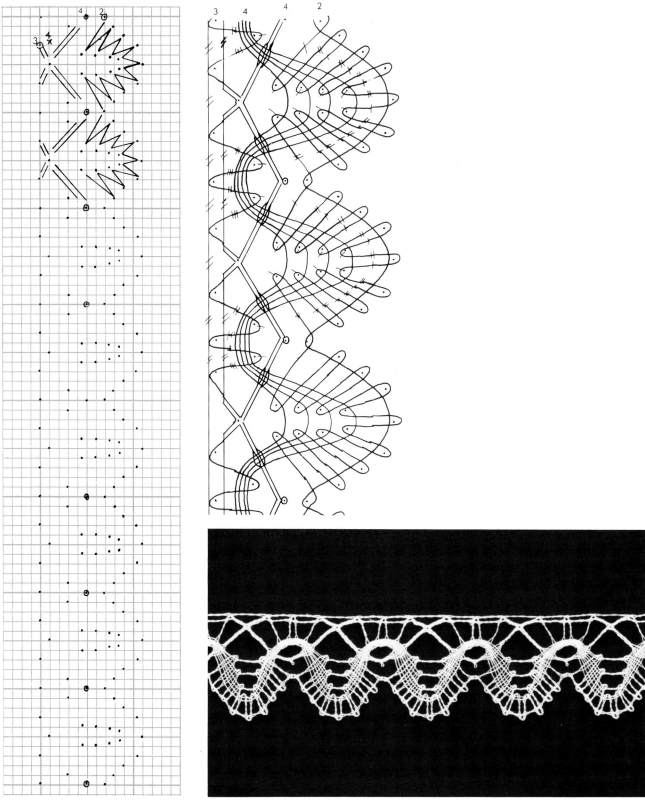

Detail
Tally
a. Using # 2 as worker (returning threads to original position) 2 twists, tally, 4 twists.
b. Using # 3 as worker (exchanging position of original threads) – hitch not necessary if sufficient twists are used

Edging–6
11 pairs + 1 gimp

Ground–Dieppe, **C**
Tally–Single tally in Dieppe ground, **A**
Fan–Gimp as Trellis fan, **D1**
Footing–WS with 2 WS passives, (variation with Torchon in between vs WS), **A2**

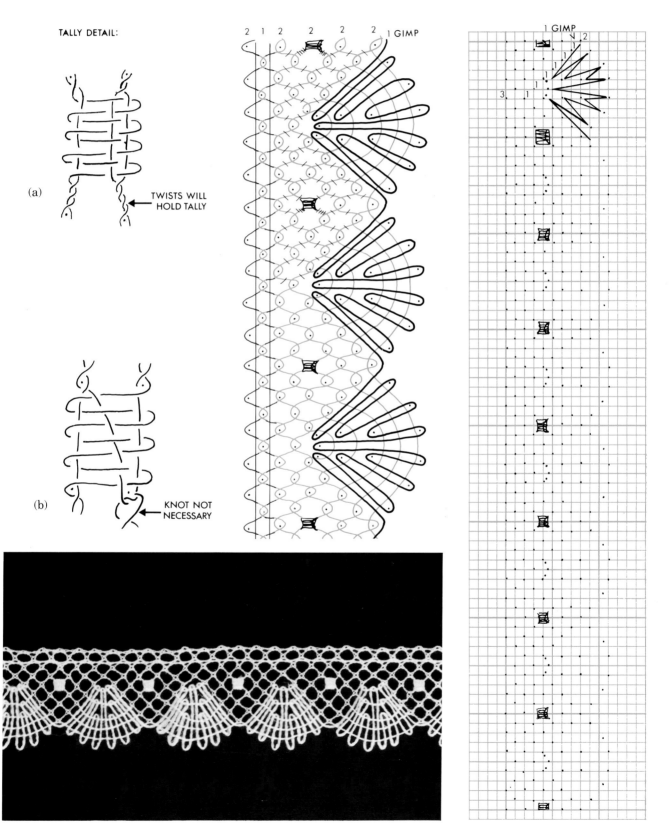

TALLY DETAIL:

(a) TWISTS WILL HOLD TALLY

(b) KNOT NOT NECESSARY

2 1 2 2 2 2 1 GIMP

1 GIMP

3 1

Edging–7
12 pairs

Stitch–WS and CS, **A, B**
Ground–Torchon, **B**
Spider–With hole, **C2**
Fan–WS, **C** (*similar to WS footing,* **A1**)
Footing–WS, **A**

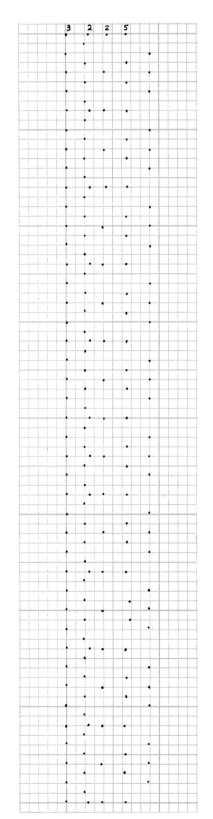

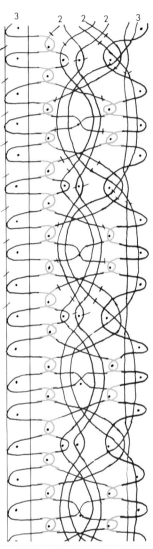

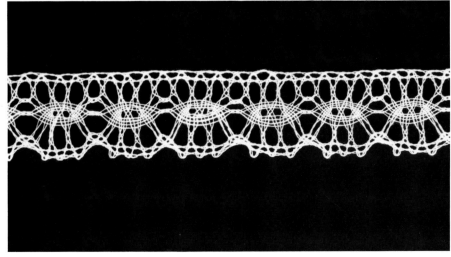

Edging–8
12 pairs + 1 gimp

Stitch–WS, **A**
Fan–Trellis with cloth and gimp, **D3**
Footing–WS with 2 WS passives, **A1**

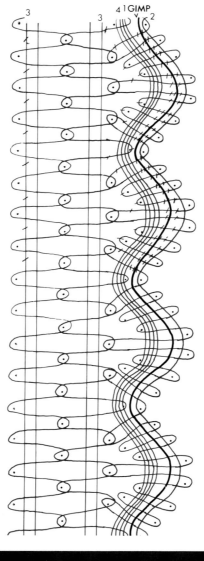

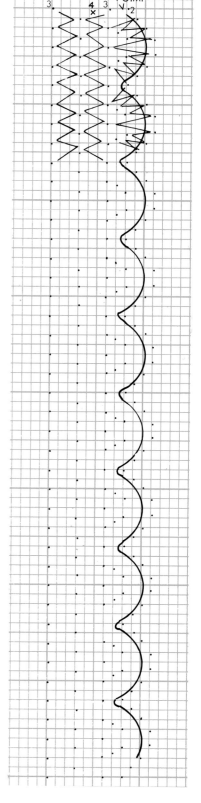

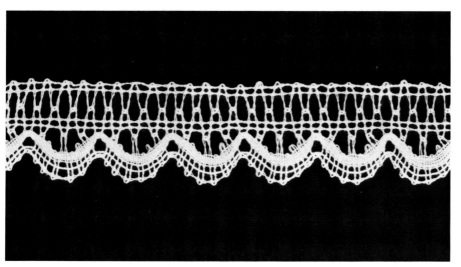

Edging–9
13 pairs + 1 gimp

Ground–Torchon, **B**
Motif–HS rectangle, **B2**
Fan–Gimp as Cloth Stitch fan (*using one pin hole*), **D** passing gimp, **B and D**
Footing–WS, **A**

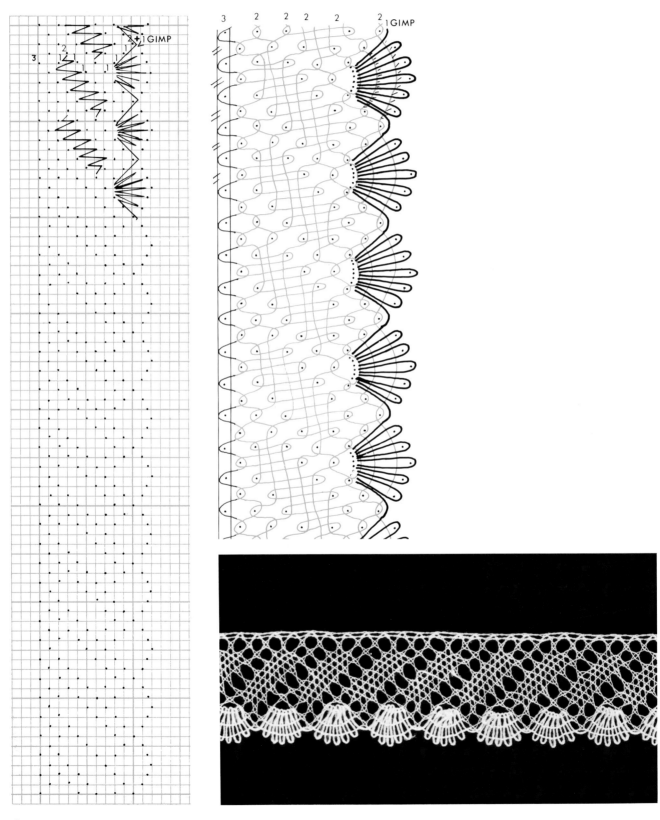

Edging–10
14 pairs

Ground–WS,.**A**
Spider–Small and Small using footing, **A** and **D2**
Fan–Double CS with WS on edge and twist, **B** and **B2**
Footing–WS with 2CS passives, **B**

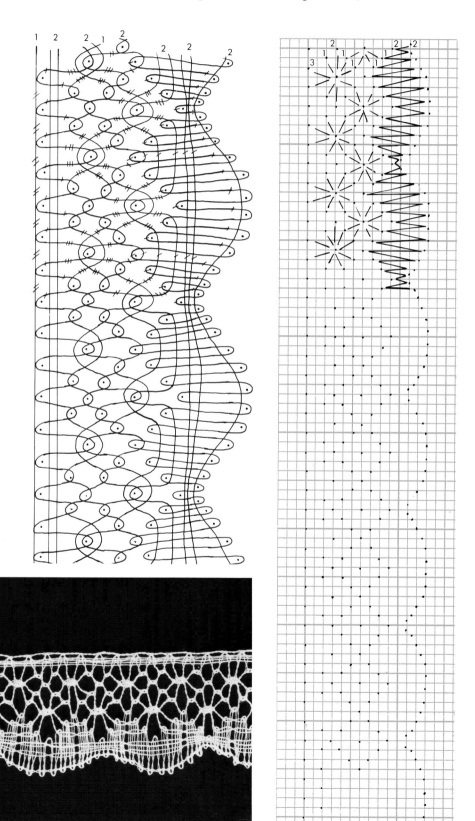

Edging–11
14 pairs

Ground–Torchon, **B**
Motif–HS window (variation), **F2**
Spider–Large using footing, **D1**
Tally–Single tally in HS ground, **A**
Fan–HS with WS at edge (*variation using HS vs CS*), **B**
Footing–WS, **A**

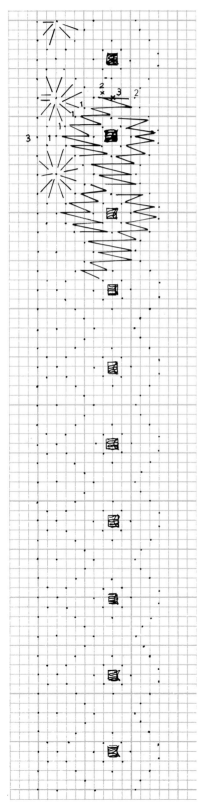

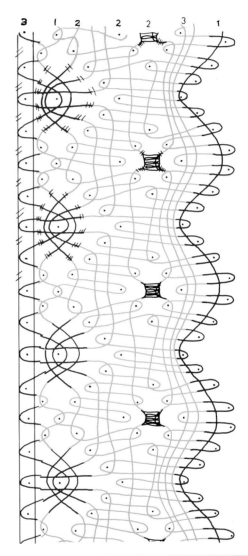

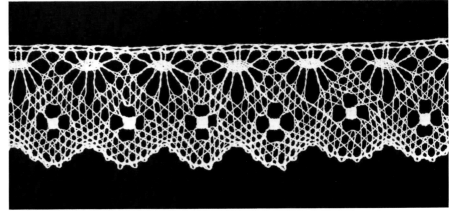

Edging–12
15 pairs

Ground–WS, **A**
Motif–CS and HS diamond, **A1** and **A2**
Spider–Small using footing, **D3** and Large with
  hole, **C1**
Fan–Trellis, **C**
Footing–Scalloped WS, **A**

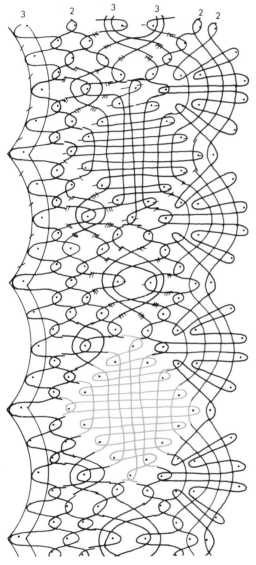

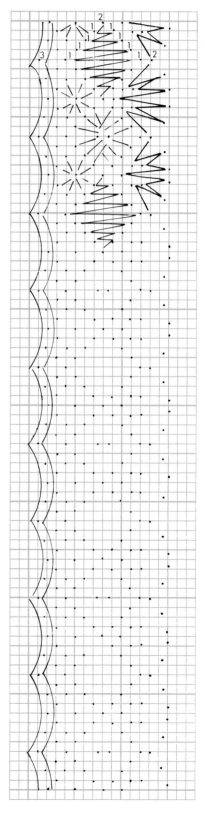

Edging–13
15 pairs

Ground–WS, **A**
Spider–With hole, **C3**
Fan–Trellis in WS, **C**
Footing–WS with WS between 2 passives **A2**

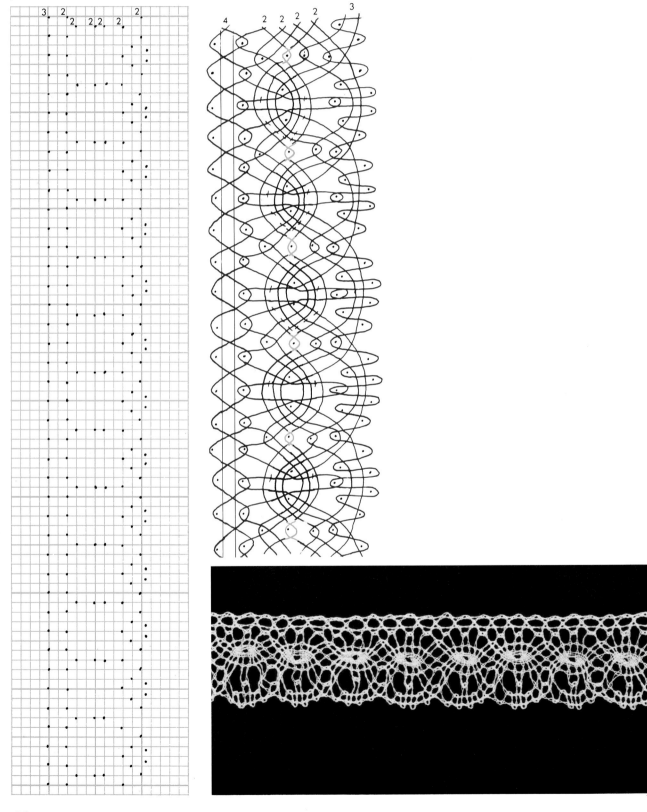

Edging–14
16 pairs

Ground–Rosepoint in Dieppe stitch, **C**
Motif–Cloth triangle, **C1**
Fan–Cloth Stitch with WS on edge and twist, **B1**
Footing–WS, **A**

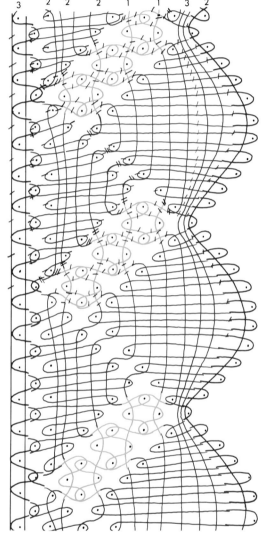

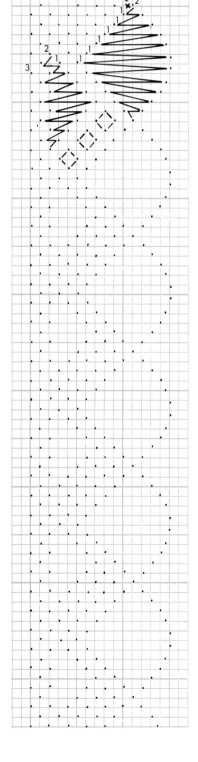

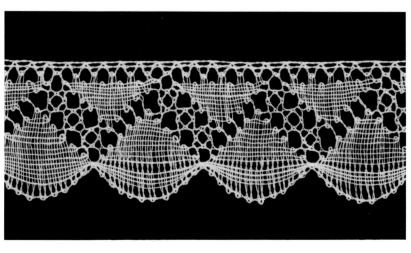

Edging–15
16 pairs + 2 gimps

Ground–Dieppe, **C**
Tally–4 tallies in Dieppe ground, **C**
Gimp–Passing one gimp, **A**
Fan–Trellis with CS, **C2**
Footing–WS with 2 CS passives, **B**

14

Edging–16
18 pairs

Ground–Rosepoint with WS corners and
 Rosepoint in Dieppe stitch with WS corners
 (variation), **B** and **C**
Motif–CS triangle, **C1**
Tally–Singles at footing, **A**
Fan–CS with twist at edge, **A**
Footing–WS, **A**

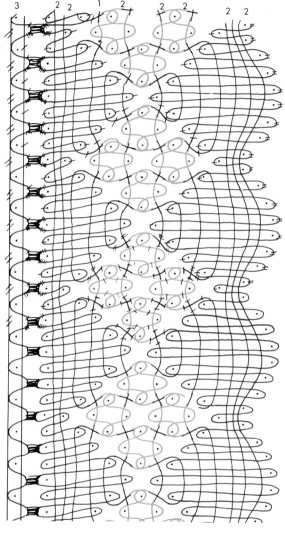

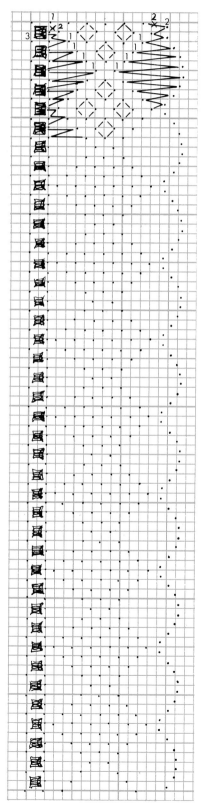

Edging–17
18 pairs

Ground–Dieppe, **C**
Motif–CS trail and Diagonal Rosepoint, **E1** and
   D2
Fan–Double Cloth Stitch with WS on edge, **B**
Footing–WS, **A**

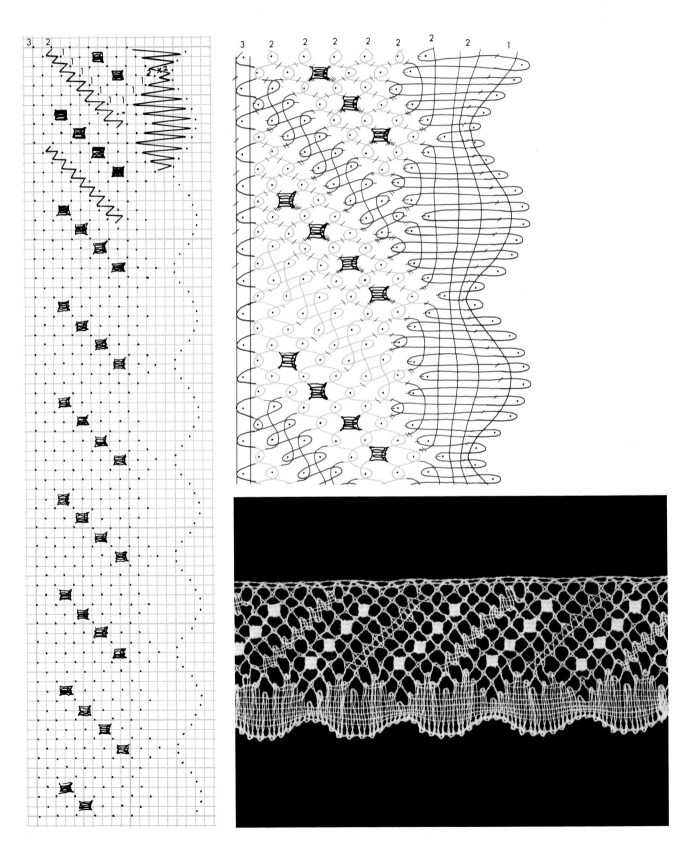

Edging–18
18 pairs

Ground–Torchon, **B**
Motif–CS trail, **E1**
Tally–Single in Torchon ground, **A**
Fan–Elongated trellis, **C3**
Footing–WS, **A**

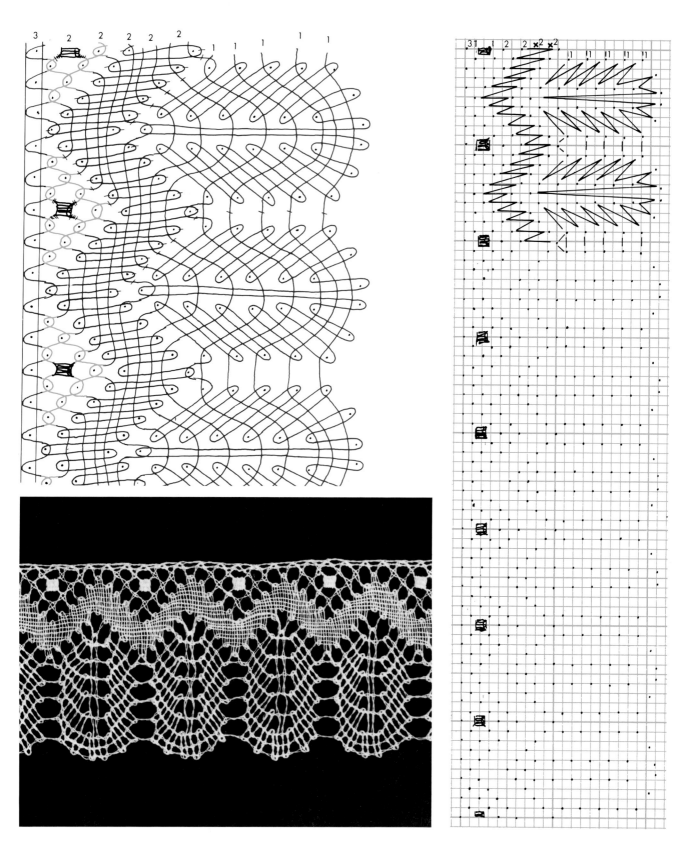

Edging–19
18 pairs

Ground–Dieppe, **C**
Motif–CS and HS diamond, **A1** and **A2**
Fan–Continuous CS with WS on edge, **B**
Footing–WS, **A**

Edging–20
19 pairs

Ground–Torchon, **B**
Motif–HS window (variation), **F2**
Spider–Large, **B**
Tally–4 tallies in HS ground, **C**
Fan–HS with WS on edge (variation using
  HS vs CS), **B**
Footing–WS, **A**

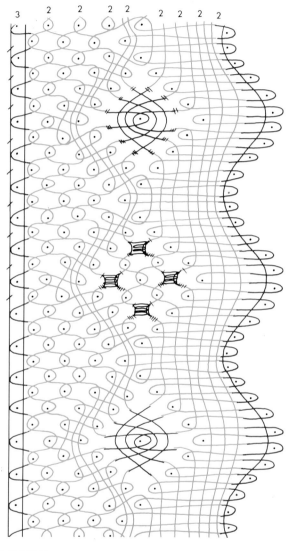

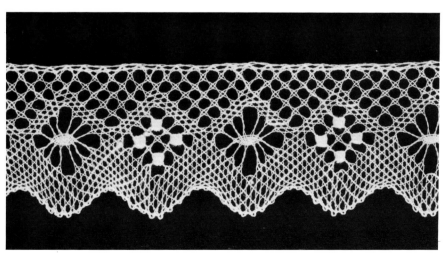

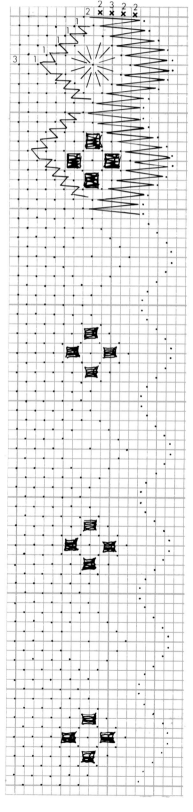

Edging–21
19 pairs

Ground–Torchon, **B**
Motif–CS chevron/heart, **D1**
Spider–Small, **A**
Fan–CS with WS on edge, **B**
Footing–WS with 2 CS passives, **B**

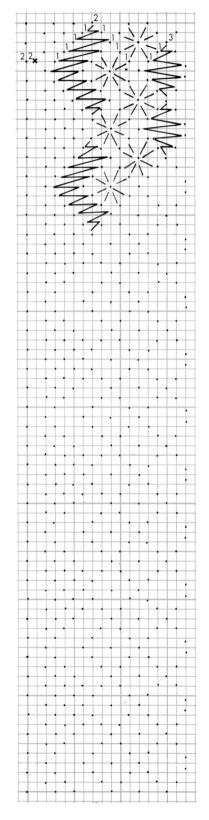

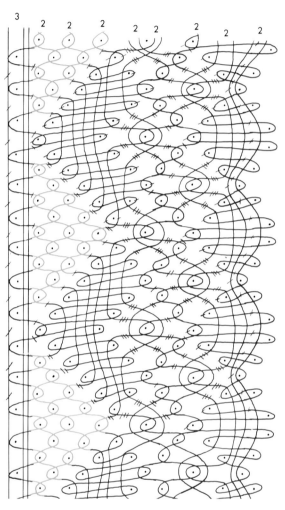

Edging–22

19 pairs + 2 pairs gimps

Ground–Torchon, **B**
Motif–HS chevron/heart (variation), **D2**
Gimp–Passing 1PG and 2PG together, **D** and **E**
Fan–Trellis with CS and gimp, **D2**
Footing–WS, **A**

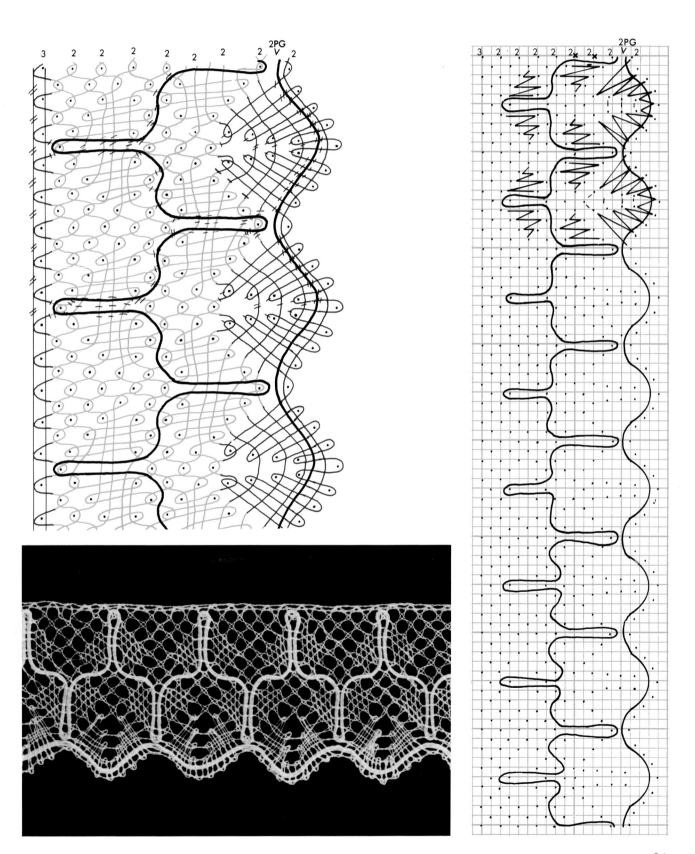

Edging–23
20 pairs

Ground–Torchon, **B**
Motif–Diagonal Rosepoint, **D1** and **D2**
Spider–Large using footing, **D2**
Fan–CS with WS on edge and twist, **B2**
Footing–WS with 2 CS passives, **B**

Edging–24
21 pairs

Ground–Torchon, **B**
Spider–Small compound, **E**
Fan–Continuous CS with WS at edge and
    twist, **B1**
Footing–WS, **A**

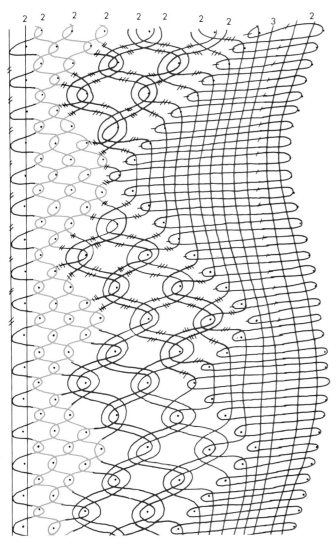

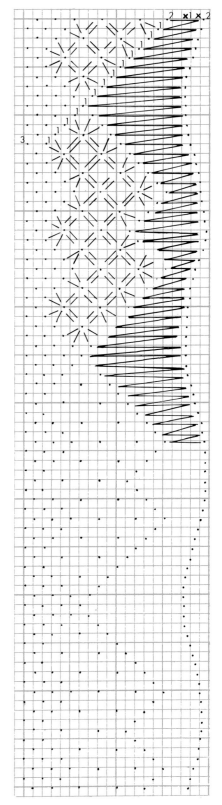

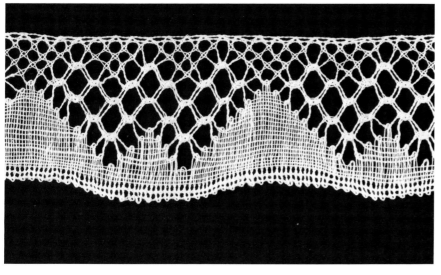

Edging–25
21 pairs

Ground–Rosepoint with WS corners, **B**
Motif–HS trail, **E2**
Spider–Large with hole, **C1**
Fan–Double CS with WS on edge, **B**
Footing–WS as Rosepoint, **A4**

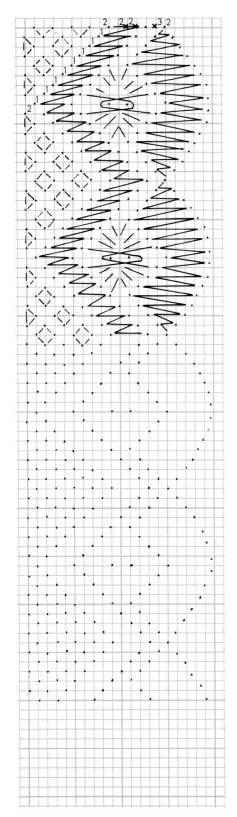

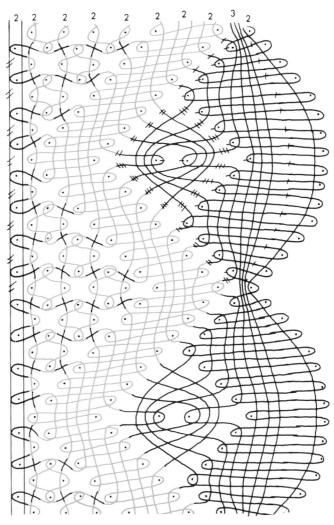

Edging–26
21 pairs

Ground–WS, **A**
Motif–CS diamond and HS trail, **A1** and **E2**
Spider–Large, **B**
Fan–Trellis, **C**
Footing–WS with 2 CS passives, **B**

Edging–27

23 pairs

(pricking p. 28)

Ground–Torchon, **B** and Simple Rosepoint, **A**
Motif–Diagonal Rosepoint, **D2** and **D2**
Fan–Trellis, **C**
Footing–WS with 2 CS passives, **B**

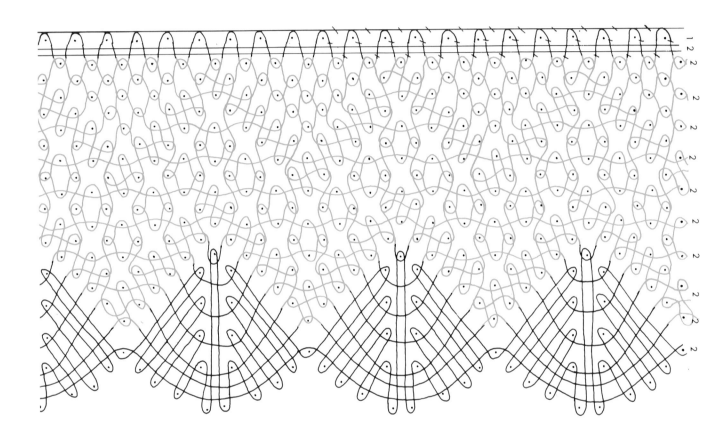

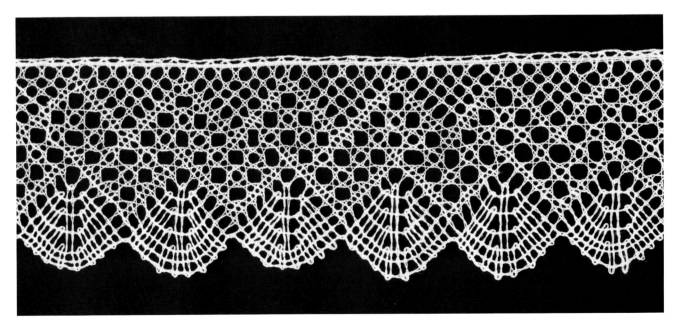

Edging–28
23 pairs
(*pricking p. 28*)

Ground–Dieppe, **C**
Motif–CS trail, **E1**
Spider–Small, **A**
Fan–Trellis, **C**
Footing–WS, **A**

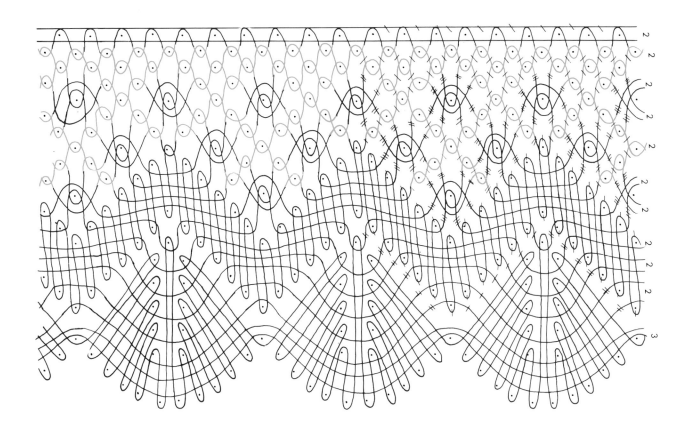

Edging–27
23 pairs
(*diagram and photo p. 26*)

Edging–28
23 pairs
(*diagram and photo p. 27*)

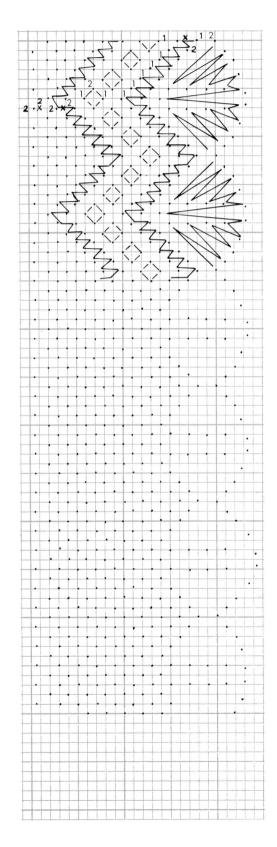

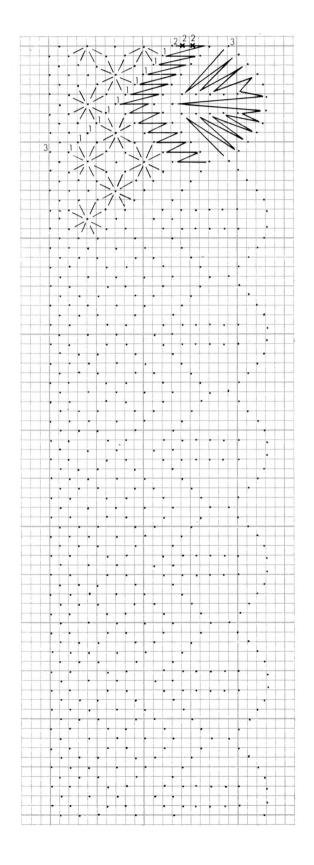

Edging–29
24 pairs
(*diagram and photo p.30*)

Edging-30
24 pairs
(*diagram and photo p.31*)

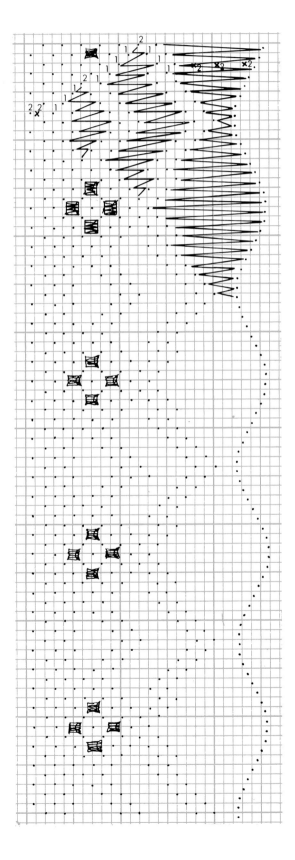

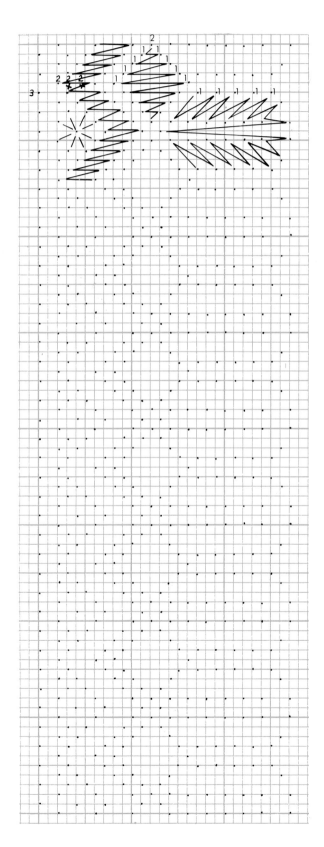

Edging–29
24 pairs
(*pricking p. 29*)

Ground–Dieppe, **C**
Motif–HS chevron (variation) and CS diamond
   (variation), **D1** and **A1**
Tally–4 Tallies in Dieppe ground, **C**
Fan–Cloth with WS on edge and twist, **B2**
Footing–WS with 2 CS passives, **B**

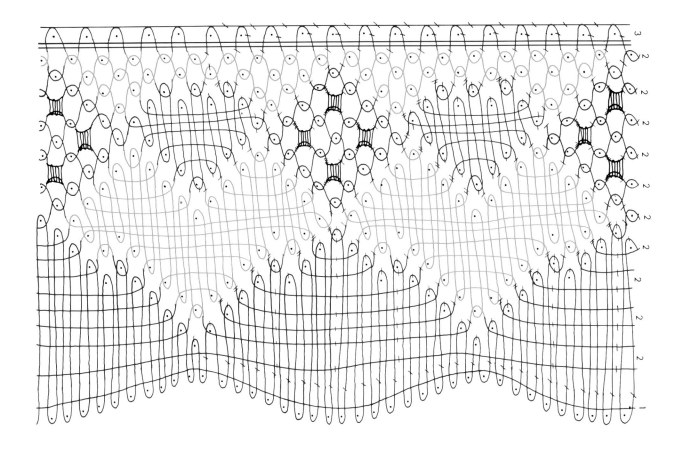

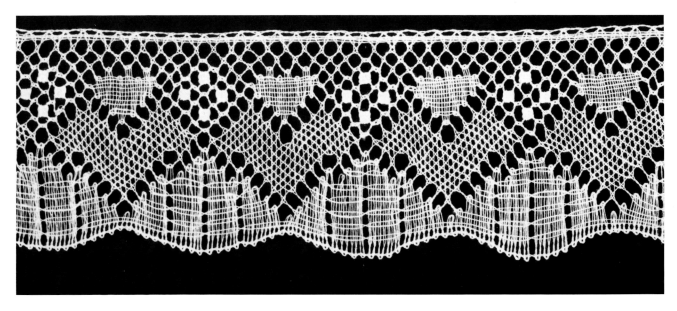

Edging–30
24 pairs
(*pricking p. 29*)

Ground–Dieppe, **C**
Motif–CS diamond, **A1** and HS trail, **E2**
Spider–Small, using sewing edge, **D3**
Fan–Elongated trellis, **C3**
Footing–WS with 2 CS passives, **B**

Edging–31
25 pairs
(*pricking p. 34*)

Ground–Dieppe, **C**
Motif–HS trail, **E2**
Tally–Single in Dieppe ground, **A**
Fan–Double CS with WS on edge, **B**
Footing–WS with 2 CS passives, **B**

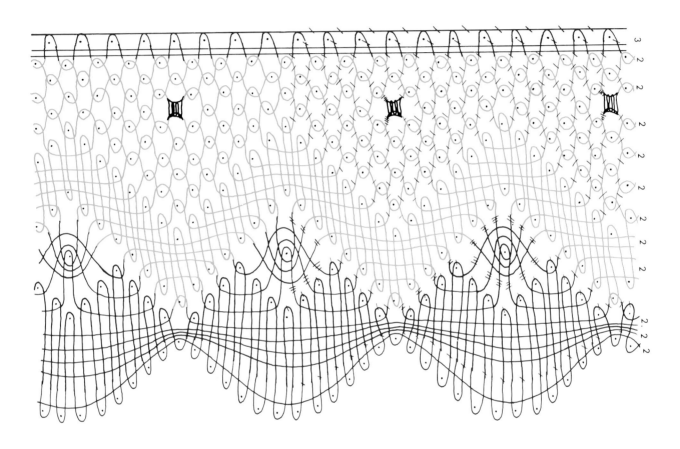

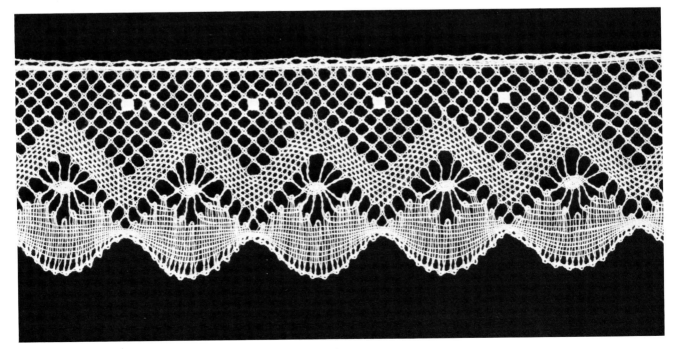

32

Edging–32
25 pairs
(*pricking p. 34*)

Ground–Dieppe, **C**
Motif–CS diamond and HS rectangle, **A1** and
  B2
Spider–Large, **B**
Fan–CS with WS on edge and trellis **B** and **C**
Footing–WS, **A**

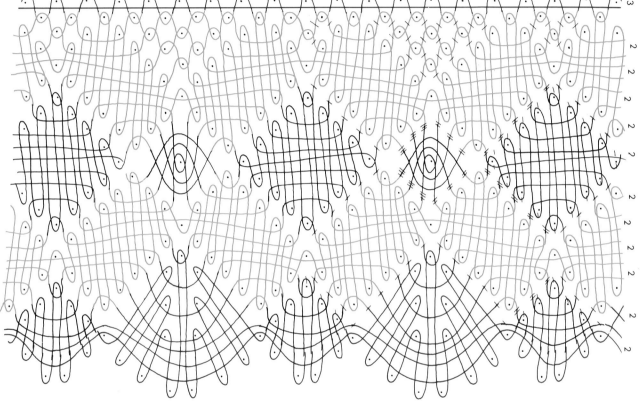

Edging–31
25 pairs
(*diagram and photo p. 32*)

Edging–32
25 pairs
(*diagram and photo p. 33*)

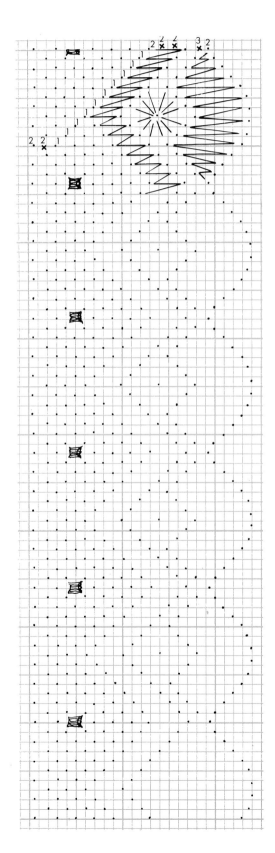

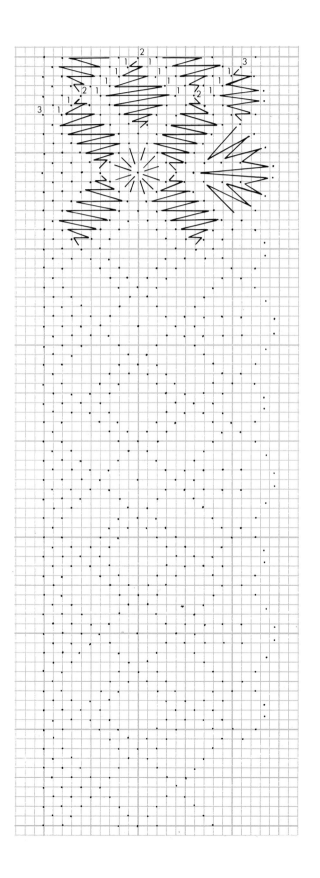

Edging–33
28 pairs
(*diagram and photo p. 36*)

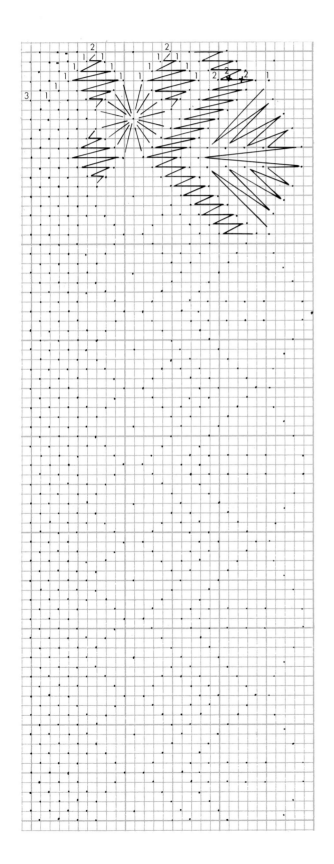

Edging–34
30 pairs
(*diagram and photo p. 37*)

Edging–33
28 pairs
(*pricking p. 35*)

Ground–Dieppe, **C**
Motif–CS diamond and CS trail, **A1** and **E1**
Spider–Large, **B**
Fan–Trellis, **C**
Footing–WS, **A**

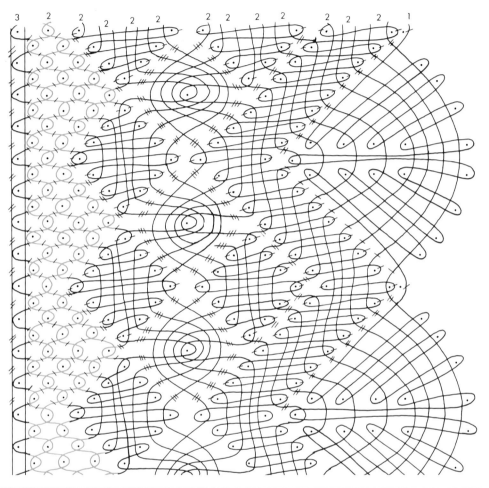

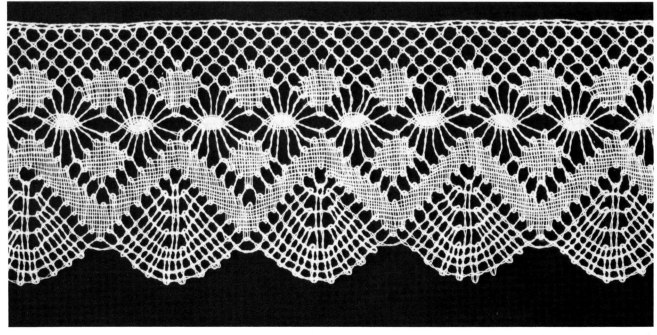

Edging–34
30 pairs
(*pricking p. 35*)

Ground–Torchon, **B**
Motif–HS trail, **E2**
Spider–Large, **B**
Fan–CS with WS on edge and twist, **B2**
Footing–WS, **A**

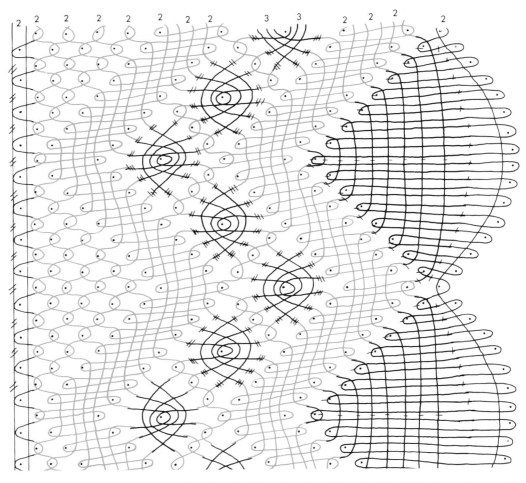

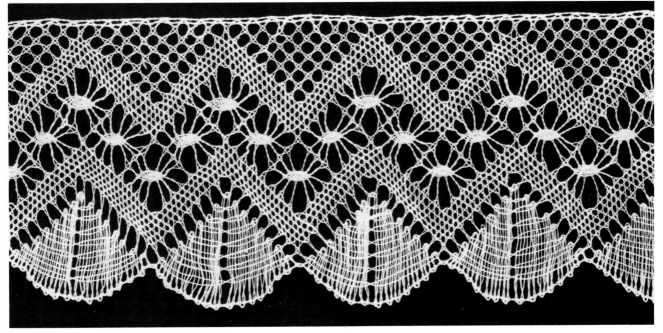

4.INSERTIONS

Insertion–1
7 pairs + 1 pair gimps

Stitch–WS, **A**
Braid–Single crossing 2G or 2PG in CS, **C**
Gimp–Passing 2G or 2PG in CS or separated
   with twists, **C** or **D**

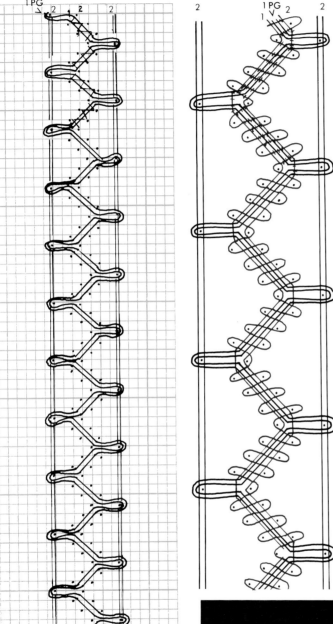

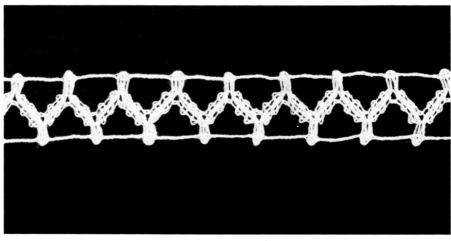

Insertion–2
8 pairs

Stitch–WS, **A**
Ground–Rosepoint in HS with WS corners, **B**
Sewing edge–WS as Rosepoint, **A4**

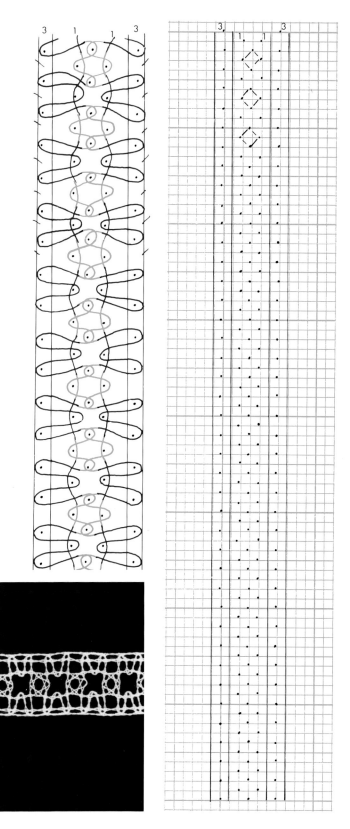

Insertion–3

8 pairs + 2 pairs gimps

Stitch–WS, **A**
Gimp–Passing 2G in CS or separated with
   twists, **C** or **D** and crossing 2PG, **F**
Sewing edge–WS, **A**

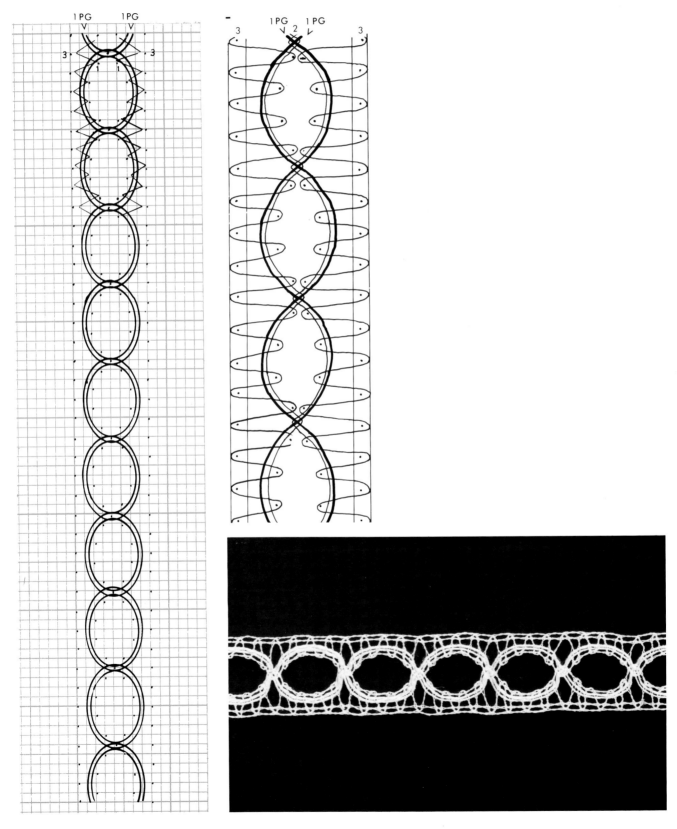

Insertion–4
10 pairs + 1 pair gimps

Stitch–WS, **A**
Ground–Torchon, **B**
Gimp–Passing 2G separately, **D**
Sewing edge–WS, **A**

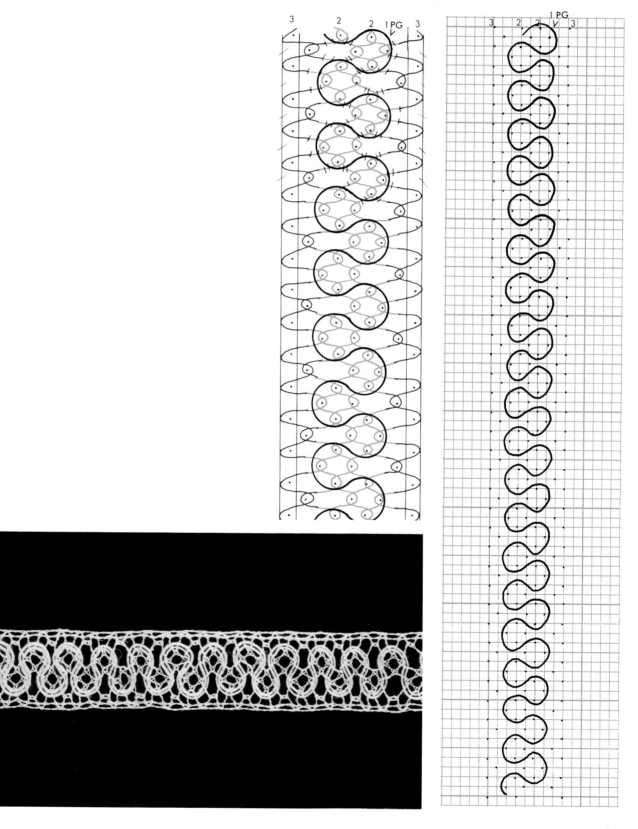

41

Insertion–5
11 pairs

Ground–Torchon, **B**
Motif–Diagonal Rosepoint, **D1** and **D2**
Tally–Single in ground, **A**
Sewing edge–WS, **A**

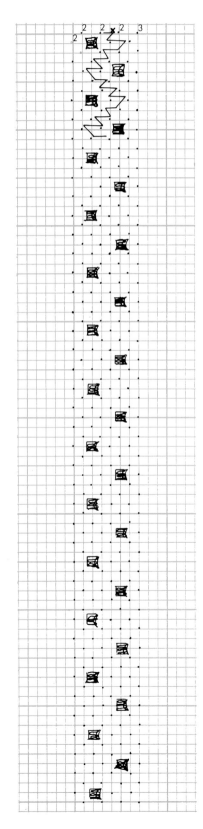

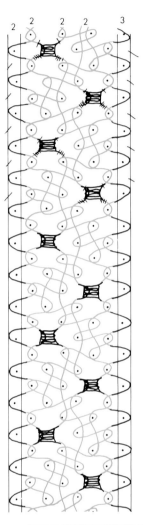

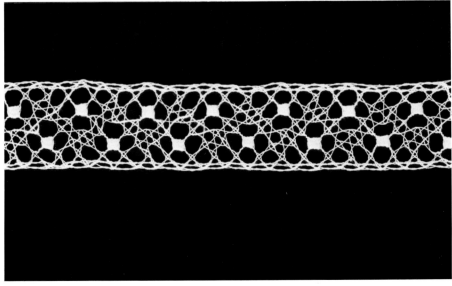

Insertion–6
12 pairs

Ground–Rosepoint with WS corners, **B**
Motif–Diagonal Rosepoint, **D1** and **D2**
Sewing edge–WS, **A** or WS as Rosepoint, **A4**

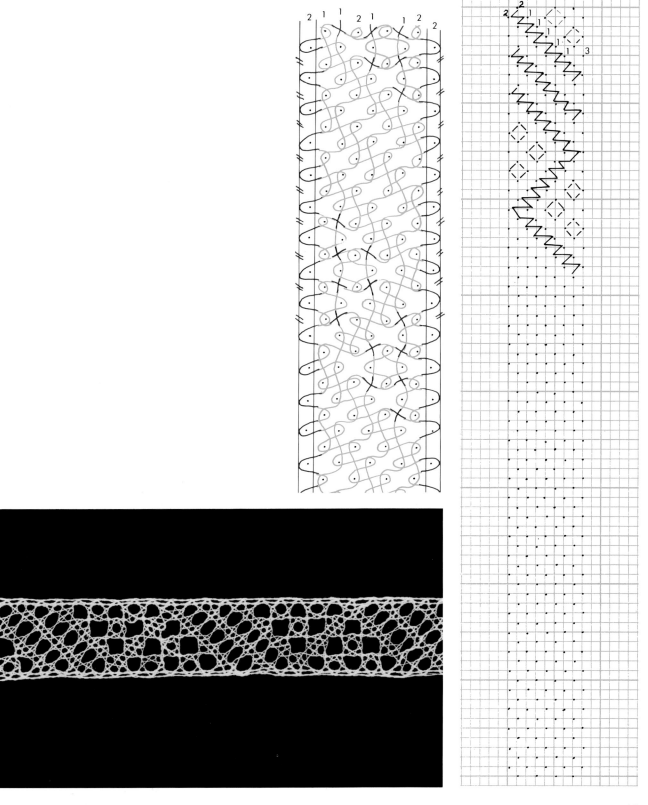

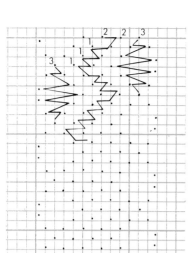

Insertion–7
13 pairs

Motif–Diagonal Rosepoint, **D1** and **D2**
Fan–Cloth with WS on edge, **B**

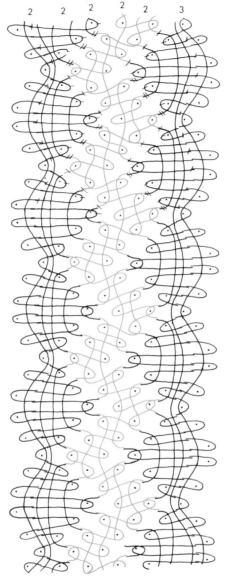

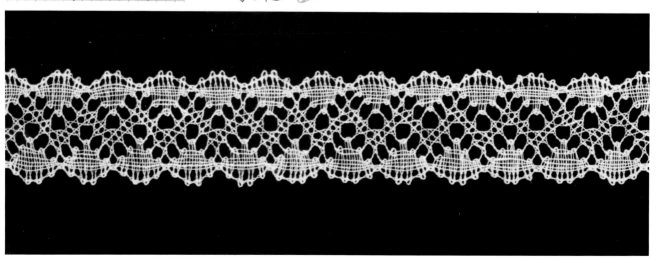

Insertion–8
14 pairs

Stitch–WS, **A**
Ground–Diagonal Rosepoint, **D2**
Motif–HS diamond, **A2**
Sewing edge–WS, **A3**

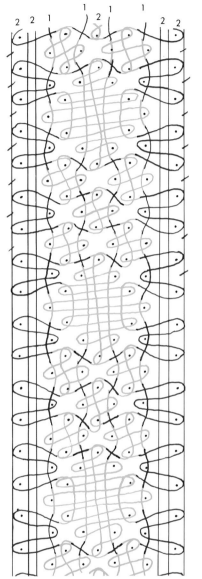

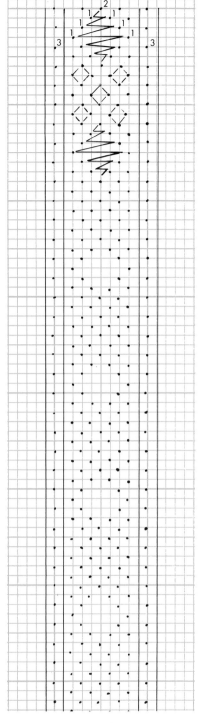

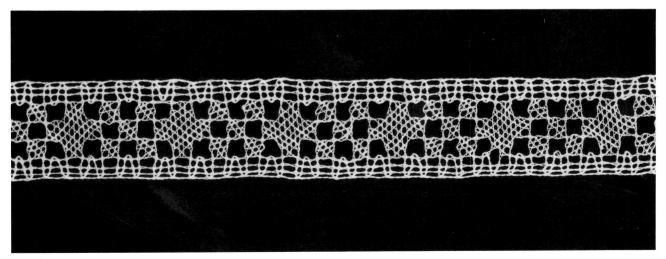

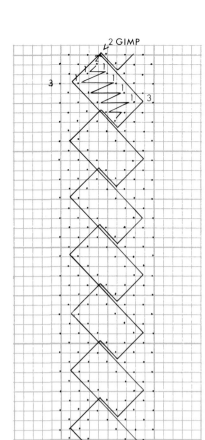

Insertion–9
14 pairs + 1 pair gimps

Ground–Dieppe, **C**
Motif–CS rectangle, **B1**
Gimp–Passing 1G, **A** and passing 2G together, **E**
Sewing edge–WS, **A**

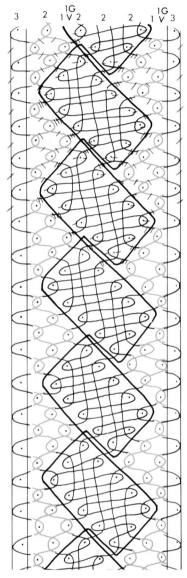

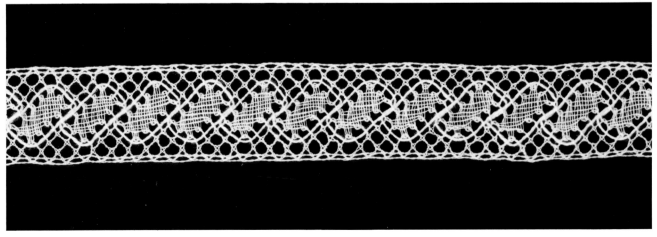

Insertion–10
16 pairs

Ground–Rosepoint in Dieppe stitch, **C**
Motif–CS triangle, **C1**
Sewing edge–WS, **A**

Detail
Rosepoint in Dieppe stitch

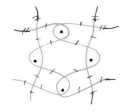

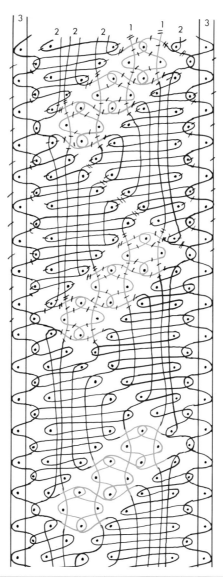

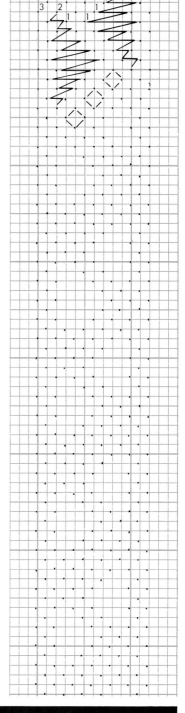

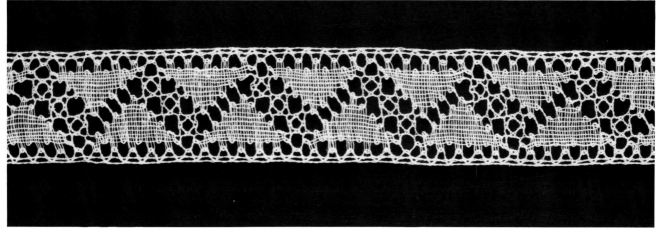

Insertion–11

16 pairs + 1 pair gimps

Ground–HS, **D** and Torchon, **B**
Gimp–Passing 1 gimp, **A** and passing 2G
  together, **E**
Sewing–HS with WS at edge, **D**

48

Insertion–12
17 pairs

Ground–WS, **A**
Motif–HS trail, **E2**
Spider–Small, using sewing edge, **D3**
Sewing edge–WS with 2 CS passives, **B**

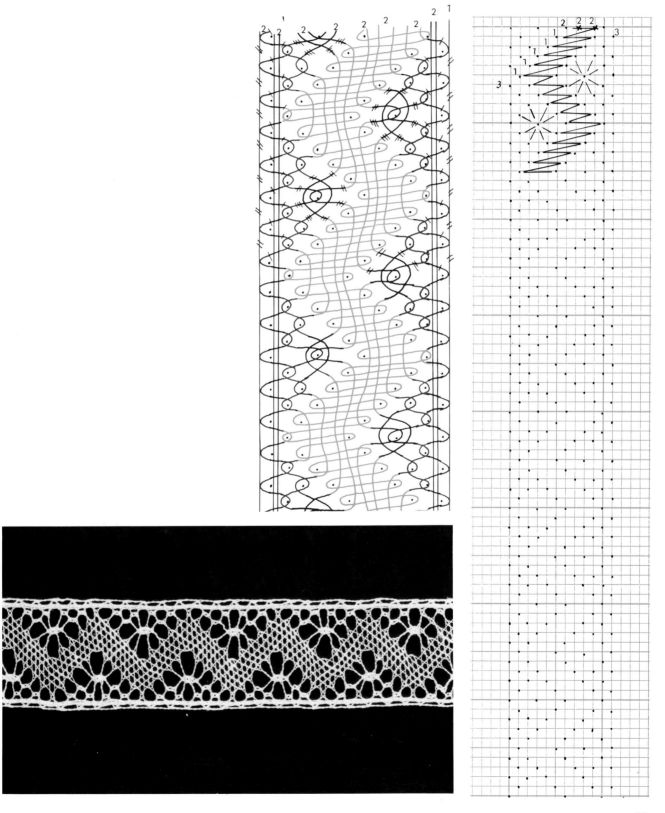

Insertion–13

17 pairs + 2 pairs gimps

Ground–Torchon, **B**
Tally–Single in Torchon ground, **A**
Gimp–Passing 2G and 2PG together, **E** and
    crossing 2PG, **F**
Sewing edge–WS, **A**

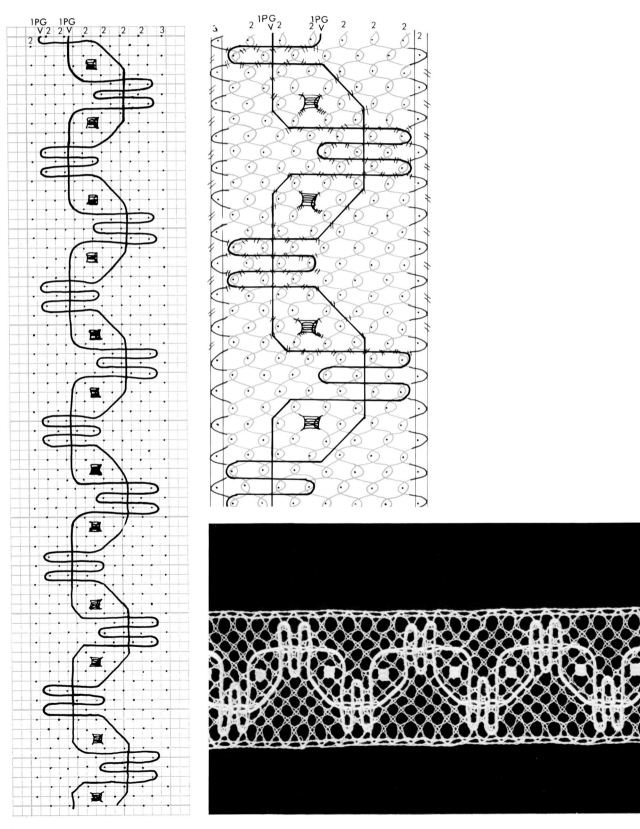

Insertion–14
18 pairs

Ground–Rosepoint in Dieppe stitch, **C**
Motif–HS diamond, **A2**
Daisy–8-point flower, 8 pairs, **C** or 4-plait
   crossing (see **Braids**), **D**
Sewing edge–WS as Rosepoint, **A4**

Insertion–15

18 pairs + 2 gimps

Stitch–WS, **A**
Gimp–Passing 1 gimp, **A**
Fan–Trellis with CS and gimp, **D3**
Sewing edge–WS, **A**

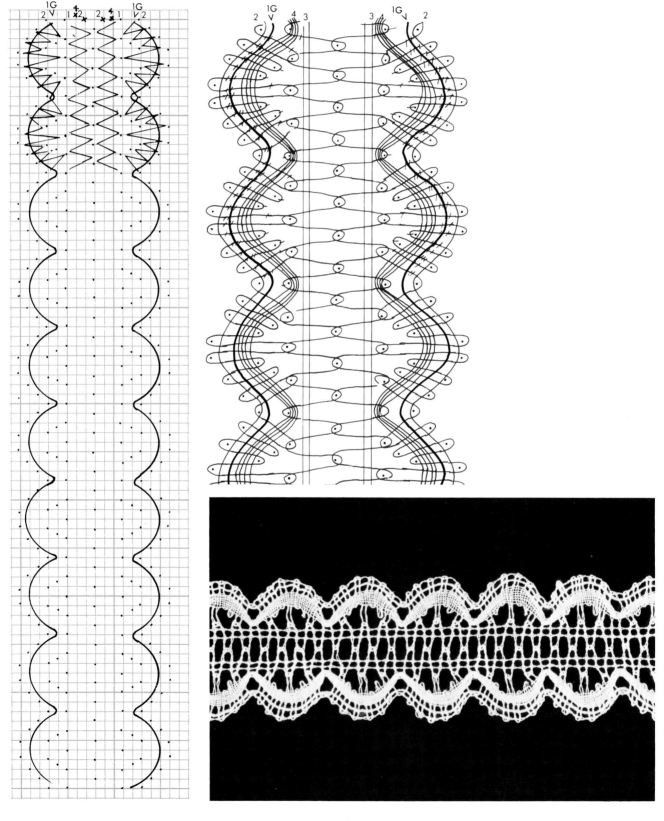

Insertion–16
22 pairs

Ground–Torchon, **B**
Motif–CS and HS chevron/heart, **D1** and **D2**
Spider–Small, **A**
Sewing edge–WS, **A**

53

Insertion–17

22 pairs

Ground–Torchon, **B**
Motif–HS triangle, **C2** (path of worker mirrored
  image – *see* Introduction, p.vi)
Spider–Large, **B**
Sewing edge–WS with 2 CS passives, **B**

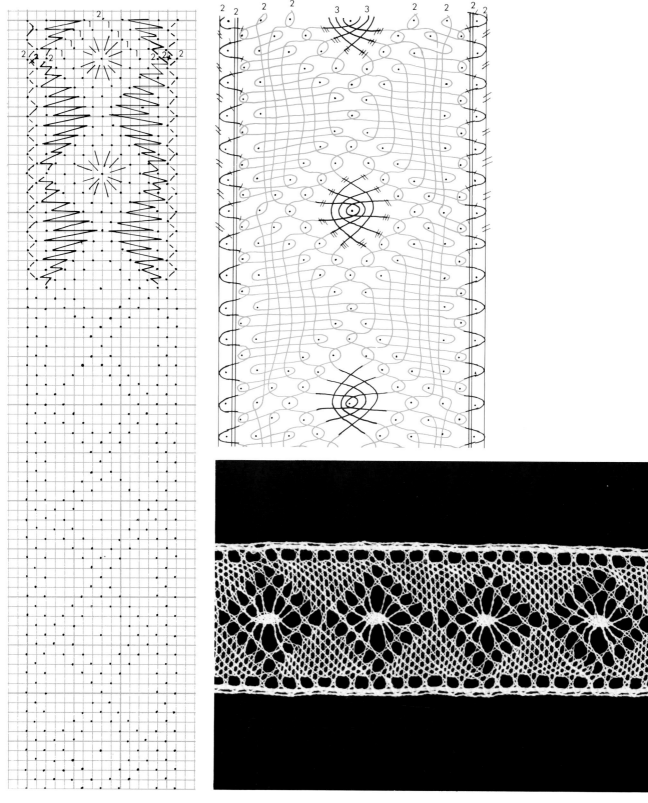

Insertion–18
22 pairs

Ground–Dieppe, **C**
Motif–CS chevron, **D1** and Diagonal Rosepoint,
D1 and **D2**
Tally–With Dieppe ground, **A**
Sewing edge–WS, **A**

Insertion–19
22 pairs

Stitch–WS, **A**
Motif–CS triangle, **C1** (path of worker mirrored
  image–*see* Introduction, p.vi)
Spider–Large compound, **E** and in cloth, **F**
Sewing edge–WS, **A**

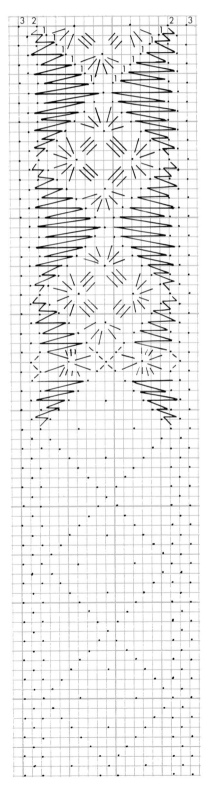

Insertion–20
23 pairs

Ground–Torchon, **B**
Motif–HS trail, **E2** or HS rectangle, **B2**
Spider–Small, **A**
Sewing edge–WS with 2 CS passives, **B**

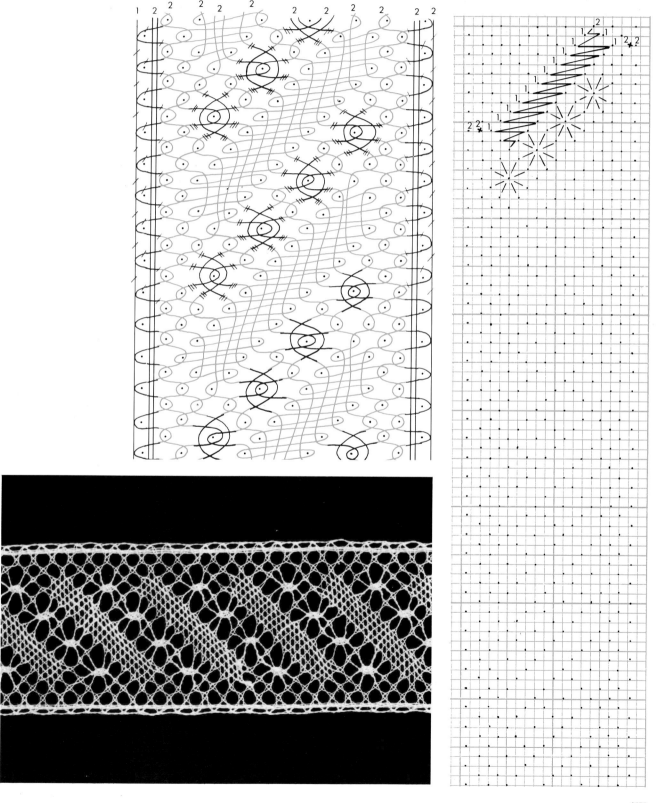

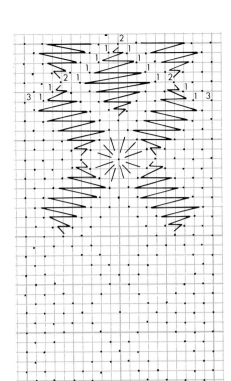

Insertion–21
24 pairs

Ground–Dieppe, **C**
Motif–Cloth diamond, **A1** and HS rectangle, **B2**
Spider–Large, **B**
Sewing edge–WS, **A**

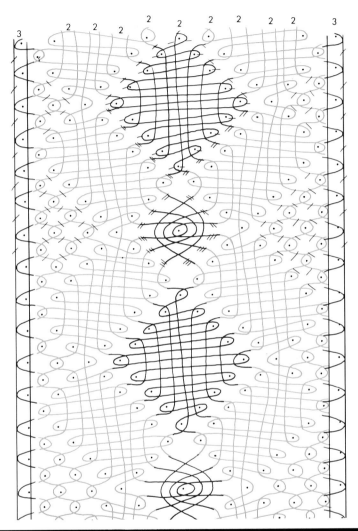

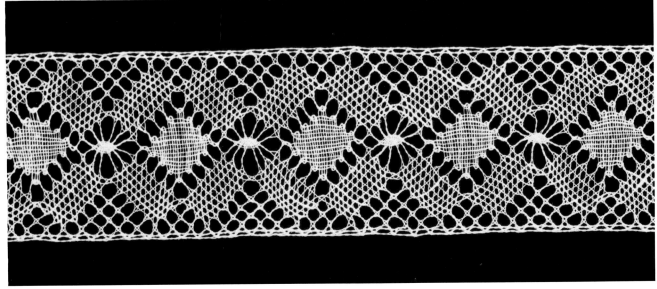

Insertion–22
24 pairs

Ground–Rosepoint with WS corners, **B**
Motif–CS and HS diamond, **A1** and **A2** and CS
   triangle, **C1** (path of worker mirrored image
   –*see* Introduction, p.vi)
Sewing edge–WS with 2 CS passives, **B**

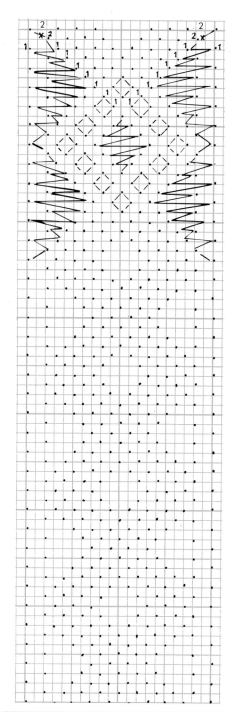

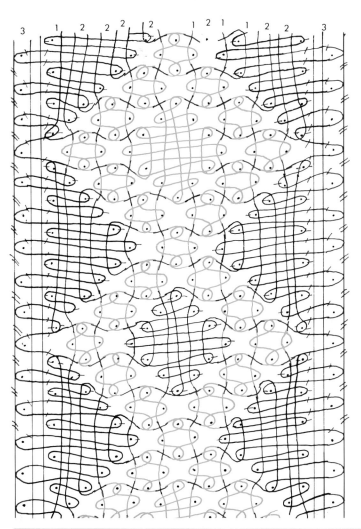

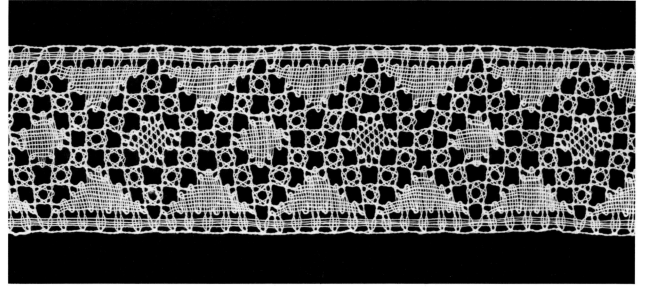

Insertion–23
24 pairs

Ground–Dieppe, **C**
Motif–HS chevron/heart, **D2**
Spider–Large, **B**
Sewing edge–WS with 2 CS passives, **B**

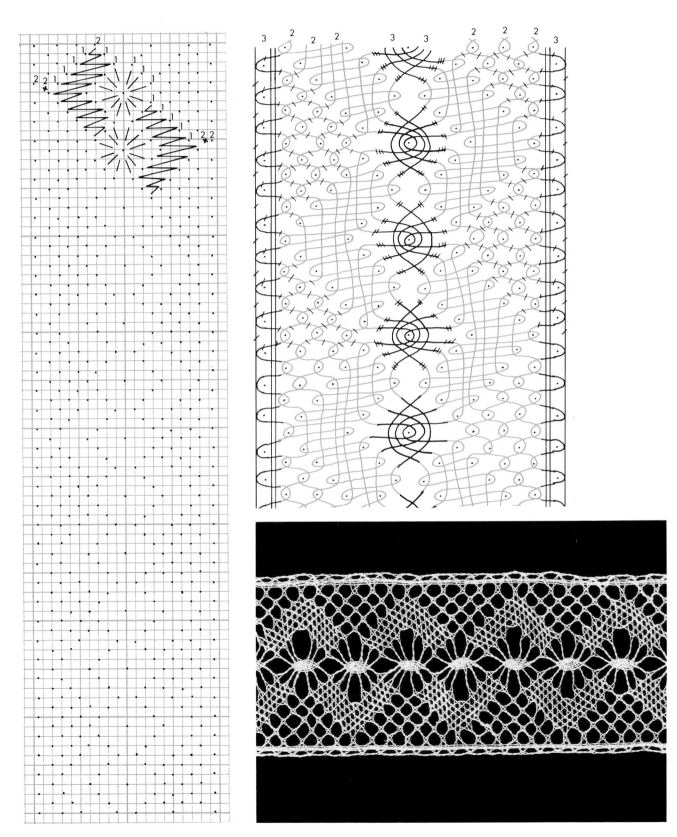

Insertion–24
24 pairs

Ground–Rosepoint in HS with WS corners, **B**
Motif–Whole and HS trail, **E1** and **E2**
Spider–Large, **B**
Sewing edge–WS as Rosepoint (variation), **A4**

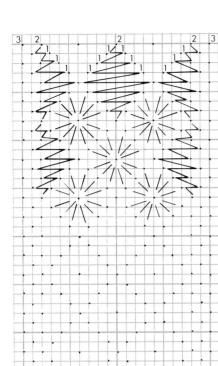

Insertion–25
24 pairs

Stitch–WS, **A**
Motif–CS diamond and triangle, **A1** and **C1**
Spider–Large, **B**
Sewing edge–WS, **A**

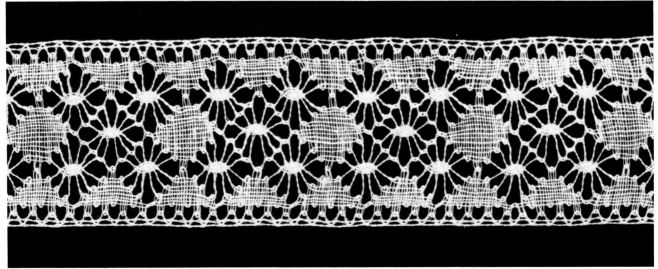

Insertion–26
26 pairs

Ground–WS, **A**
Spider–Small, using sewing edge, **D3**/Large
   with hole, **C1** and Double, **G**
Tally–With WS ground, **A**
Sewing edge–WS with 2 CS passives, **B**

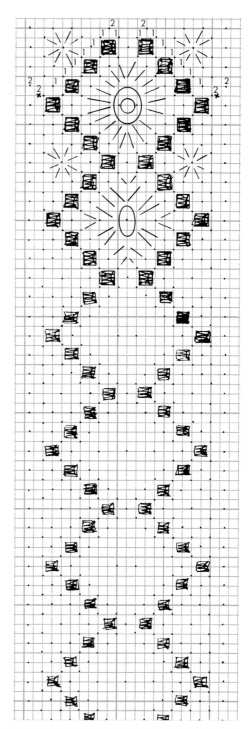

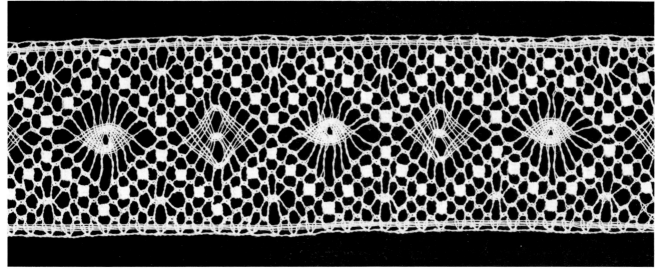

Insertion–27
26 pairs + 2 pairs gimps
(*pricking p.66*)

Ground–Torchon, **B**
Motif–Diagonal Rosepoint, **D1** and **D2**
Tally–Single in Torchon ground, **A**
Gimp–Passing 2PG or 2G together in CS, **E** or
   passing 2PG or 2G separated by twists, **D**
Sewing edge–WS, **A**

This pattern was designed and used for the TVA commission – 3 panels (8 feet x 32 feet) for a six-story atrium space in Chattanooga, Tennessee

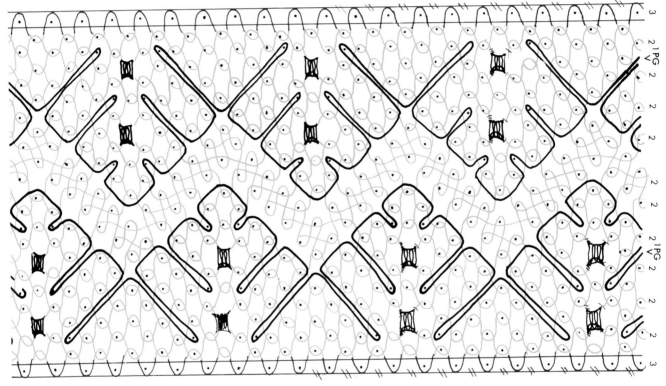

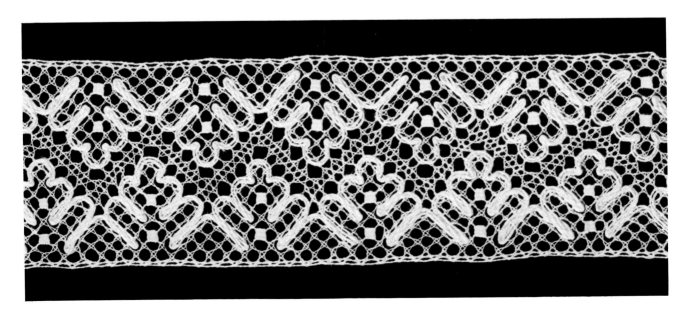

Insertion–28
28 pairs
(*pricking p.66*)

Stitch–WS at sewing edge, **A**
Ground–Dieppe, **C**
Motif–HS trail, **E2** (*creating window*)
Tally–Single in Dieppe ground, **A**
Daisy–10-point flower/10 pairs, **D** or 5-plait
   crossing, **E** (see **Braids**)
Sewing edge–WS with 2 WS passives, **A3**

Insertion–27
26 pairs + 2 pairs gimps
(*diagram and photo p. 64*)

Insertion–28
28 pairs
(*diagram and photo p. 65*)

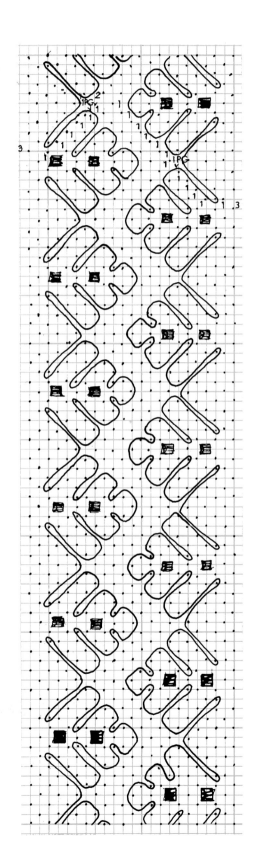

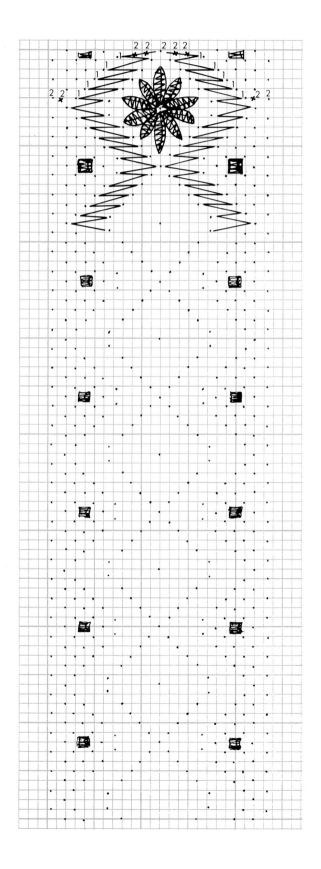

Insertion–29
28 pairs
(*diagram and photo p. 68*)

Insertion–30
28 pairs
(*diagram and photo p. 69*)

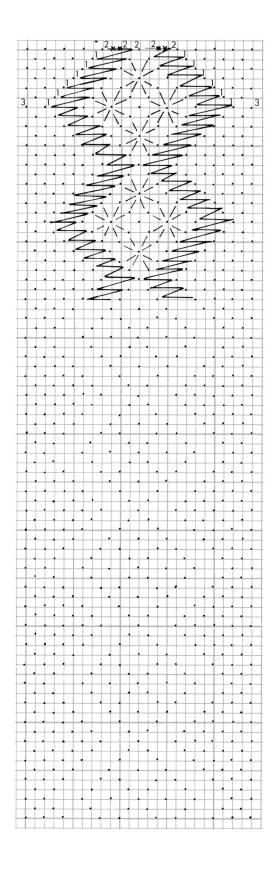

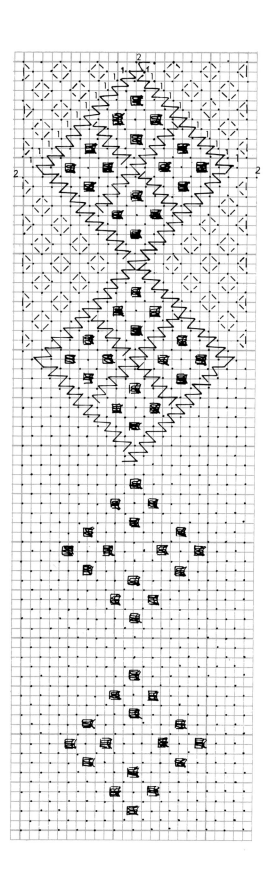

Insertion–29

28 pairs
(*pricking p. 67*)

Ground–Torchon, **B**
Motif–CS trail, **E1** (*creating window*)
Spider–Small, **A**
Sewing edge–WS, **A**

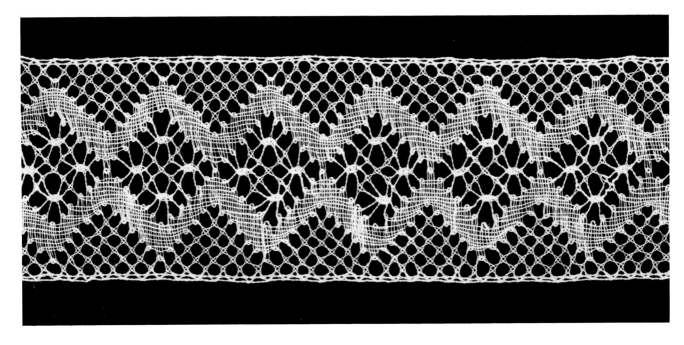

Insertion–30
28 pairs
(*pricking p. 67*)

Ground–Simple Rosepoint, **A**
Motif–Diagonal Rosepoint, **D1** and **D2**
Tally–4 tallies in ground, **C**
Sewing edge–WS as Rosepoint, **A4**

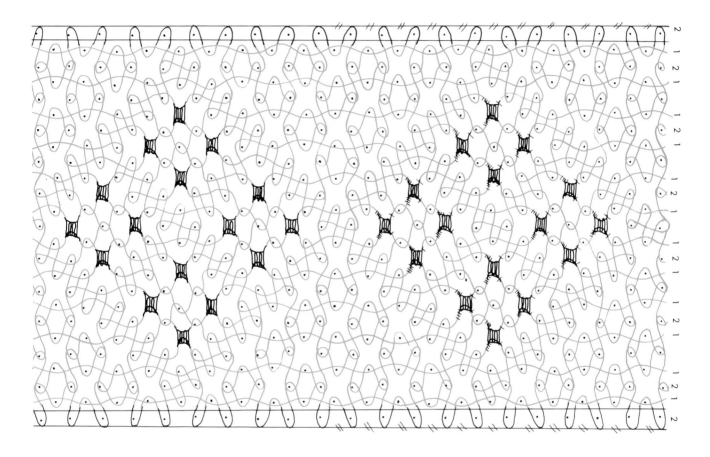

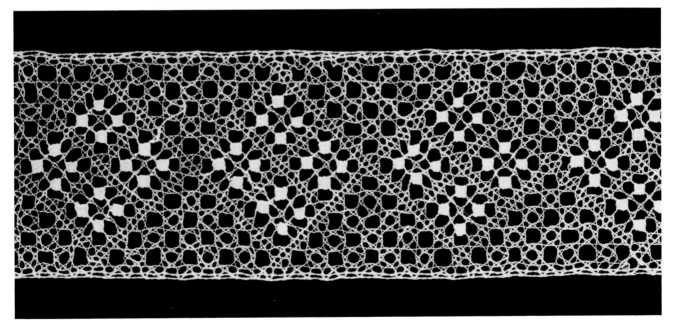

Insertion–31

29 pairs
(*pricking p. 72*)

Stitch–WS, **A**
Ground–Dieppe, **C**
Motif–CS diamond, **A1** and HS trail, **E2**
Spider–Small, **A**
Sewing edge–WS, **A**

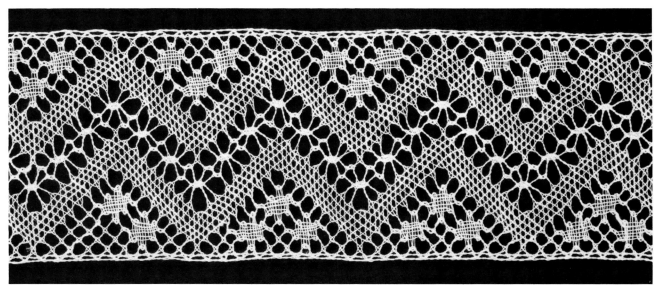

Insertion–32

30 pairs

(*pricking p. 72*)

Stitch–WS, **A**
Ground–Dieppe, **C**
Motif–CS diamond, **A1** and HS trail, **E2**
Spider–Large, **B**
Sewing edge–WS with 2 CS passives, **B**

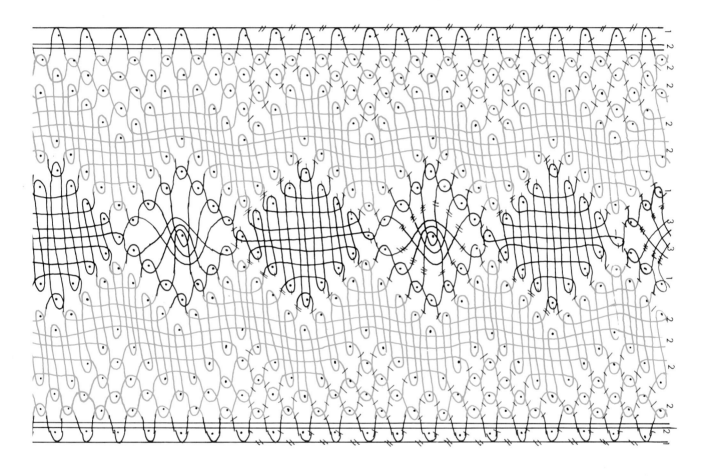

Insertion–31
29 pairs
(*diagram and photo p. 70*)

Insertion–32
30 pairs
(*diagram and photo p. 71*)

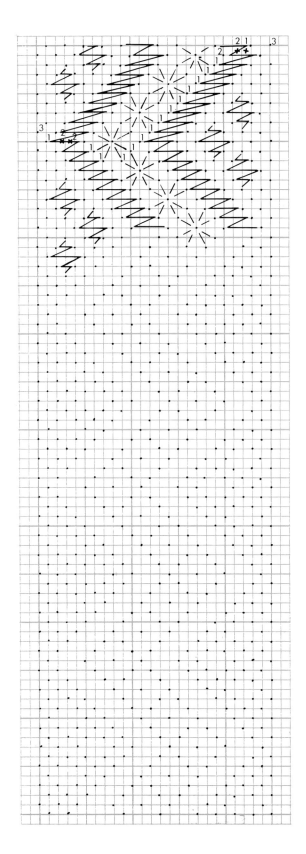

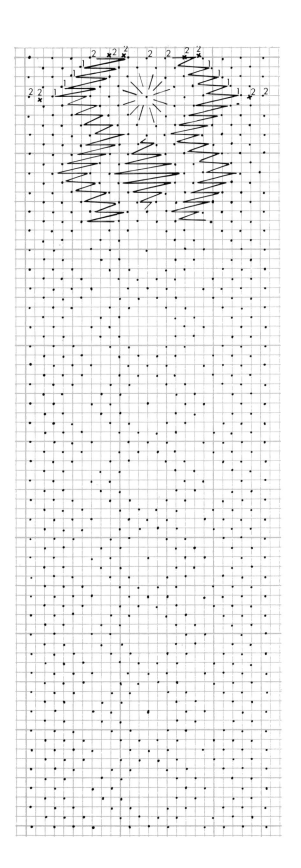

Insertion–33
32 pairs
(*diagram and photo p. 74*)

Insertion–34
36 pairs
(*diagram and photo p. 75*)

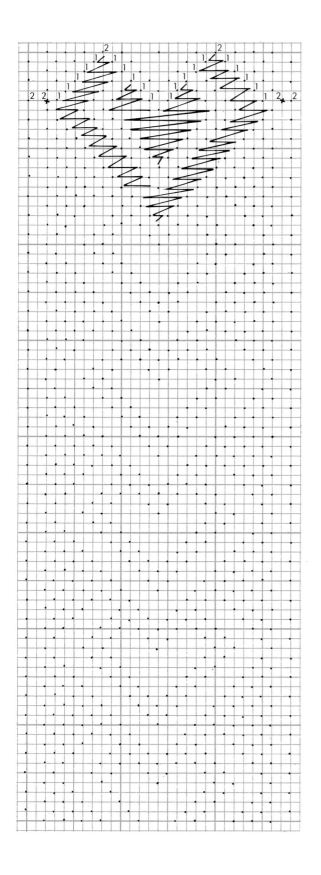

Insertion–33
32 pairs
(*pricking p. 73*)

Ground–Dieppe, **C**
Motif–CS and HS chevron/heart, **D1** and **D2**
Sewing edge–WS with 2 CS passives, **B**

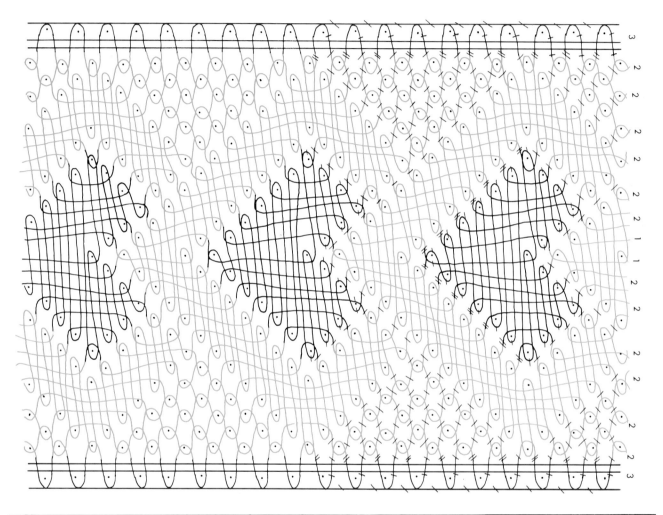

Insertion–34
36 pairs
(*pricking p. 73*)

Ground–Torchon, **B**
Motif–Diagonal Rosepoint, **D1** and **D2**
Spider–Large, **B**
Sewing edge–WS, **A**

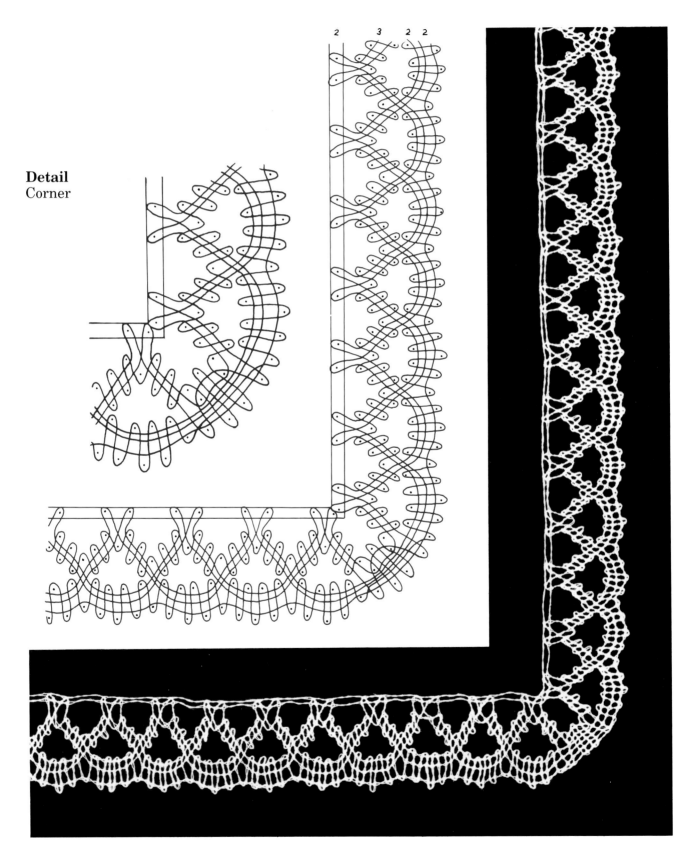

5.CORNERS

Corner–1
9 pairs
(*pricking p. 78*)

Stitch–WS, **A**
Fan–WS, **C** (*see* Detail *below*)
Footing–WS, **A**

Detail
Corner

Corner–2
21 pairs
(*pricking p. 78*)

Ground–Torchon, **B**
Motif–HS rectangle, **B2**
Spider–Large, **B**
Tally–Single in ground, **A**
Fan–Trellis with CS, **C2**
Footing–WS, **A**

Corner–1
9 pairs
(*diagram and photo p. 76*)

Corner–2
21 pairs
(*diagram and photo p. 77*)

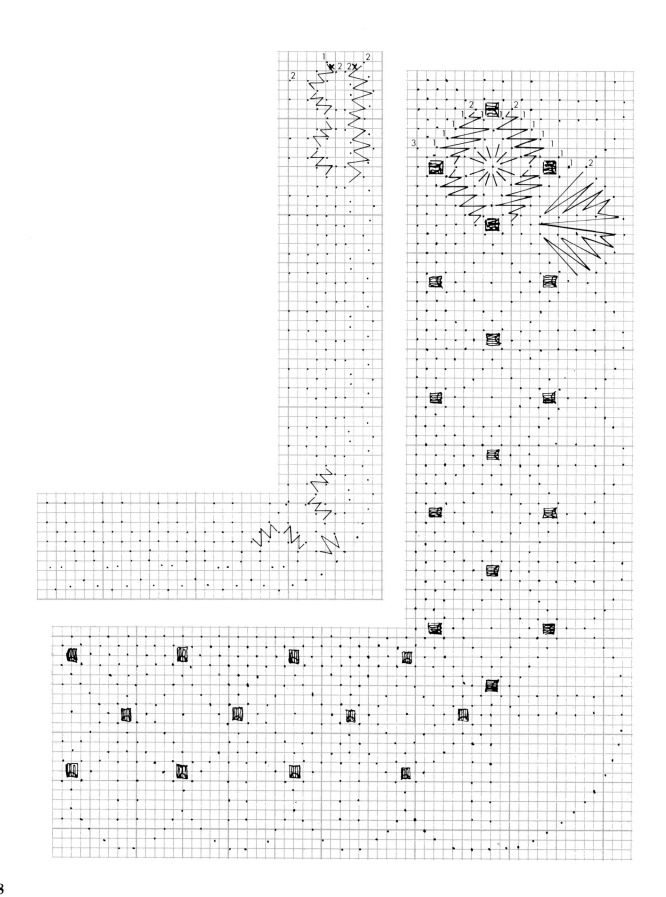

78

Corner–3
9 pairs
(*diagram and photo p. 80*)

Corner–4
21 pairs
(*diagram and photo p. 81*)

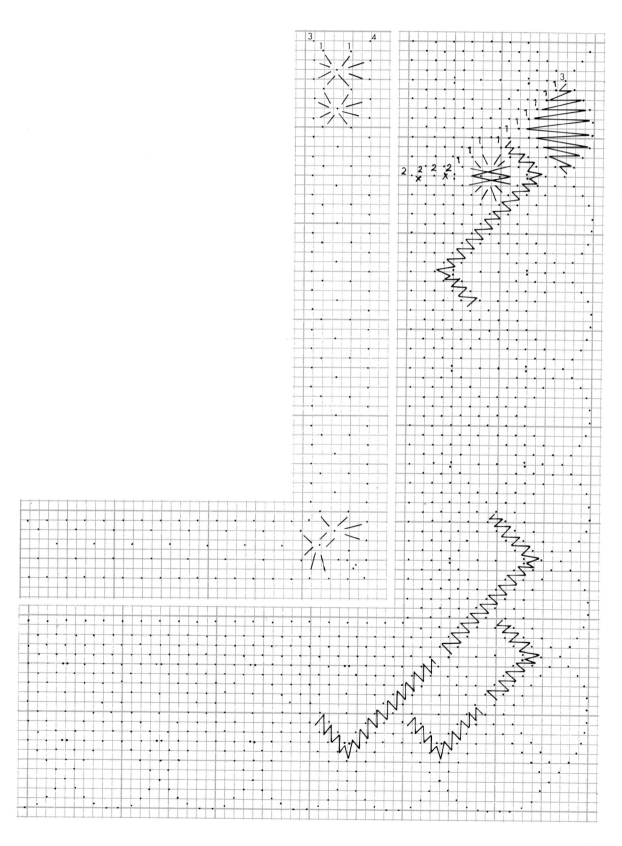

Corner–3
9 pairs
(*pricking p. 79*)

Stitch–WS, **A** and CS, **B**
Spider–Small, using sewing edge, **D4**
Sewing edge–WS with 2 WS passives, **A1** and
WS with 2 CS passives, **B1**

Detail
Corner

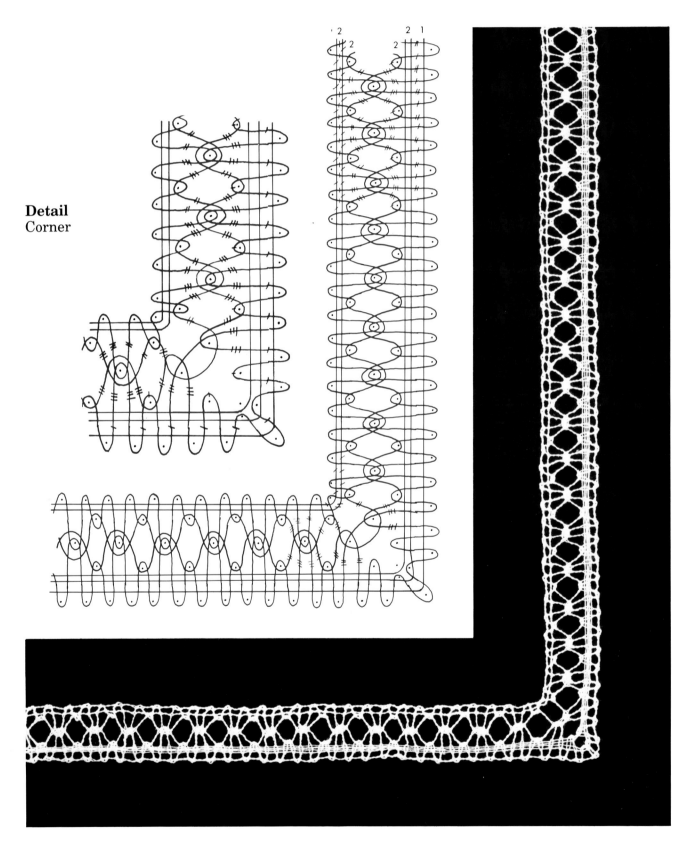

Corner–4
21 pairs
(*pricking p. 79*)

Ground–WS, **A**
Motif–CS and Diagonal Rosepoint (variation),
  E1, D1 and **D2** (using pin hole twice at corner)
Spider–With hole, **C3**
Braid–2 single at corner, **A**
Fan–CS with WS at edge and twist, **B2**
Footing–WS with 2 CS passives, **B**

Corner–5

14 pairs

(*pricking p. 84*)

Motif–CS triangle (variation), **C1**
Braid–Single (or 2 pairs), **A**
Sewing edge–WS, **A**

Detail
Corner

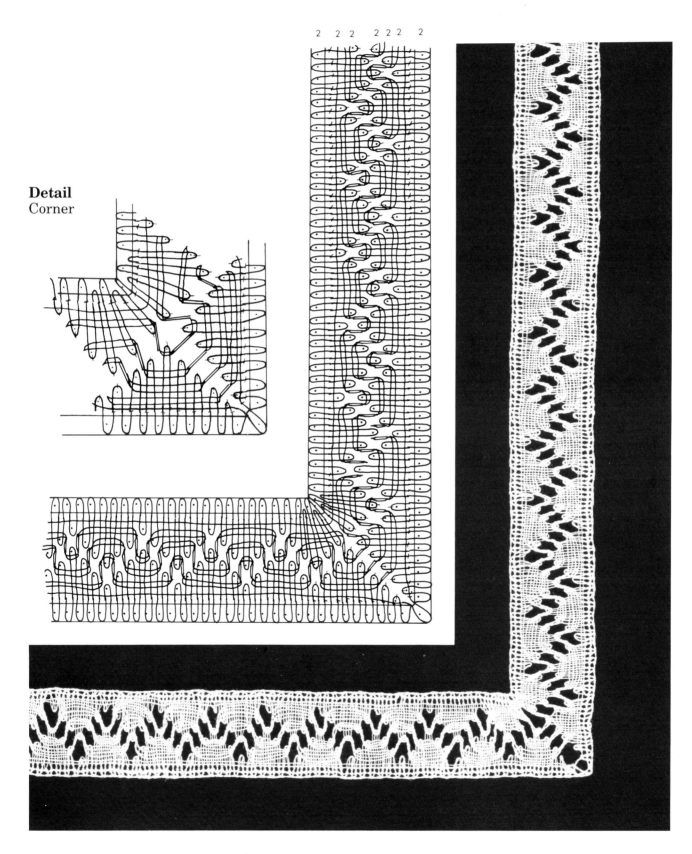

Corner–6
21 pairs
(*pricking p. 84*)

Ground–Torchon, **B**
Motif–HS trail, **D2**
Spider–Small, **A** and Small using footing, **D3**
Fan–Trellis, **C**
Footing–WS, **A**

Corner–5
14 pairs
(*diagram and photo p. 82*)

Corner–6
21 pairs
(*diagram and photo p. 83*)

Corner–7
14 pairs
(*diagram and photo p. 86*)

Corner–8
22 pairs
(*diagram and photo p. 87*)

Corner–7
14 pairs
(*pricking p. 85*)

Ground–Rosepoint with WS corners, **B**
Motif–CS triangle, **C1**
Sewing edge–WS and WS as Rosepoint, **A4**

Detail 1
Inner corner

Detail 2
Outer corner

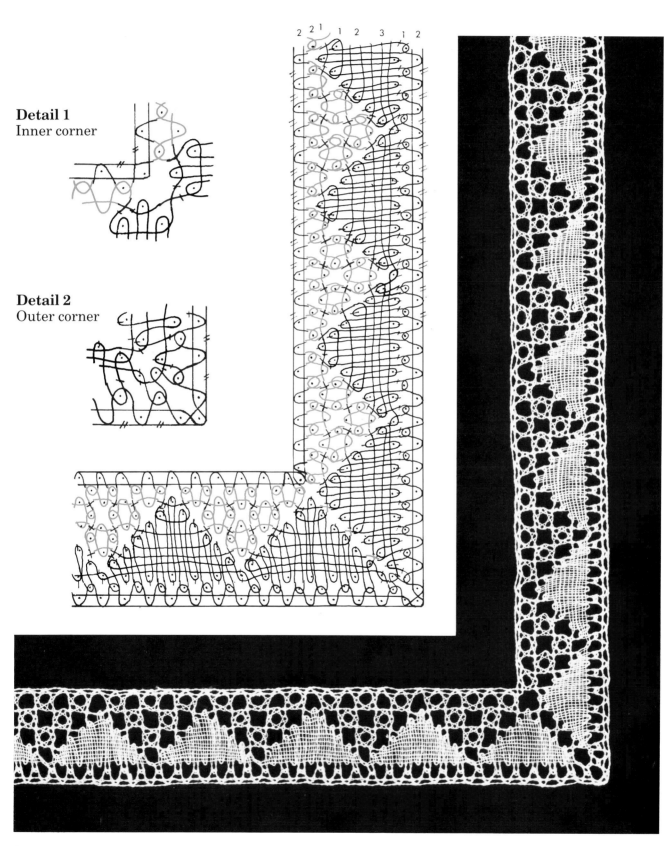

Corner–8
22 pairs
(*pricking p. 85*)

Ground–Dieppe, **C**
Motif–Diagonal Rosepoint, **D1** and **D2** and CS
diamond, **A1**
Tally–Diagonal in Dieppe stitch, **B**
Fan–WS trellis and CS with WS and twist,
C and **B2**
Footing–WS with 2 CS passives, **B**

Corner–9
17 pairs
(*pricking p. 90*)

Ground–Dieppe, **C**
Motif–CS chevron/heart, **D1**
Sewing edge–WS with 2 CS passives, **B**

Detail 1
Inner corner

Detail 2
Outer corner

2 2 2 2 2   2   2 3

Corner–10
21 pairs*
(*pricking p. 90*)

*Diagram has extra pinhole
in ground requiring 22 pairs

Ground–Dieppe, **C**
Motif–Diagonal Rosepoint, **D1** and **D2** and CS
  chevron/heart, **D1**
Fan–Trellis, **C**
Footing–WS with 2 CS passives, **B**

Corner–9
17 pairs
(*diagram and photo p. 88*)

Corner–10
21 pairs
(*diagram and photo p. 89*)

Corner–11
18 pairs + 1 pair gimps
(*diagram and photo p. 92*)

Corner–12
22 pairs
(*diagram and photo p. 93*)

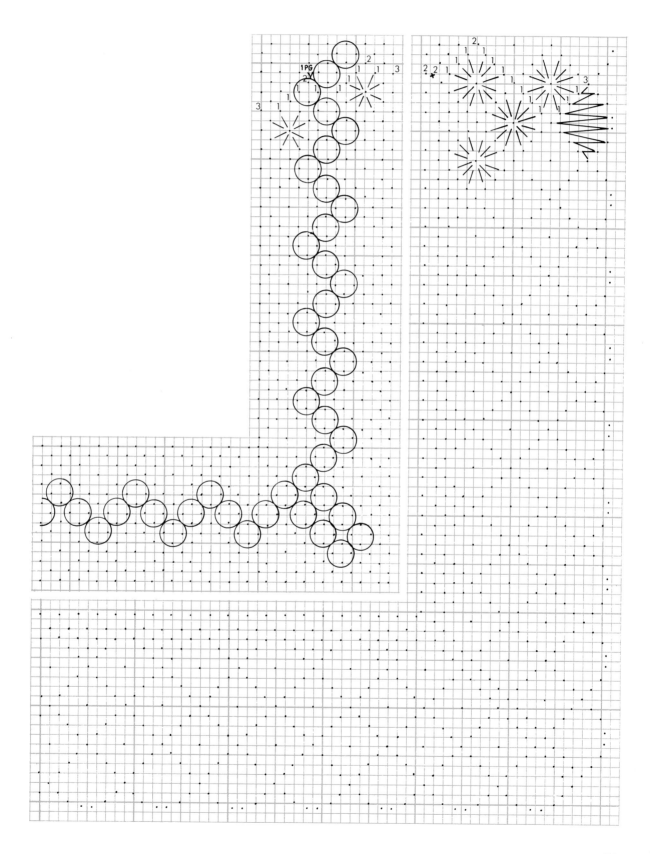

Corner–11
18 pairs + 1 pair gimps
(*pricking p. 91*)

Ground–Torchon, **B**
Spider–Small using sewing edge, **D3**
Gimp–Passing 1G, **A** and passing 2G together, **E**
Sewing edge–WS, **A**

Corner–12
22 pairs
(*pricking p. 91*)

Ground–WS, **A**
Spider–Large, **B**
Braid–Two single at corner, **A**
Fan–CS with WS at edge, **B**
Footing–WS with 2 CS passives, **B**

6. BOOKMARKS

Bookmark–1
10 pairs

Motif–HS diamond, **A2**
Fan–Cloth with WS and twist, **B1**
   and **B2** (*can use 1 pin hole,* see p. 2)
Start–Simple using HS or WS, **A2**
Ending–Pairs on outside (*exchanging worker*), **A**

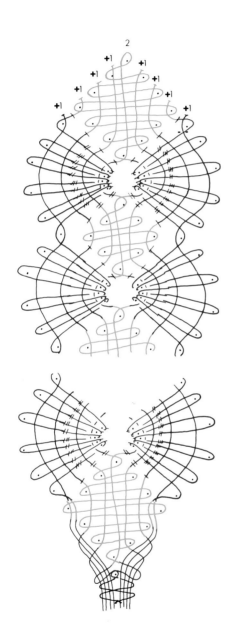

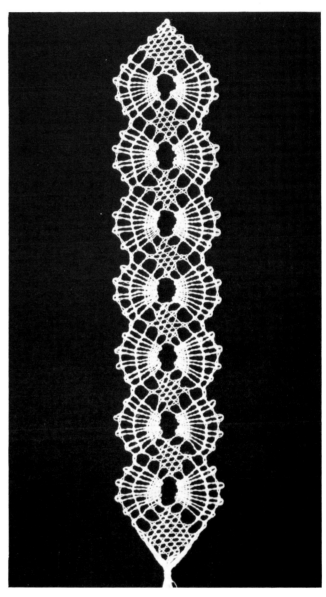

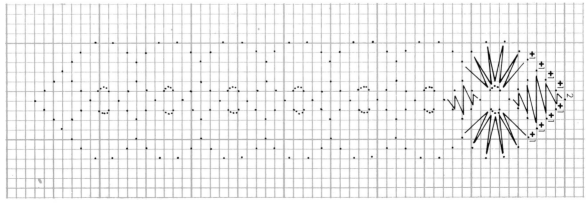

Bookmark–2
14 pairs

Motif–HS trail, **E2**
Fan–Trellis, **C**
Start–Simple in HS, **A2**
Ending–With pairs outside (*exchanging worker*), **A**

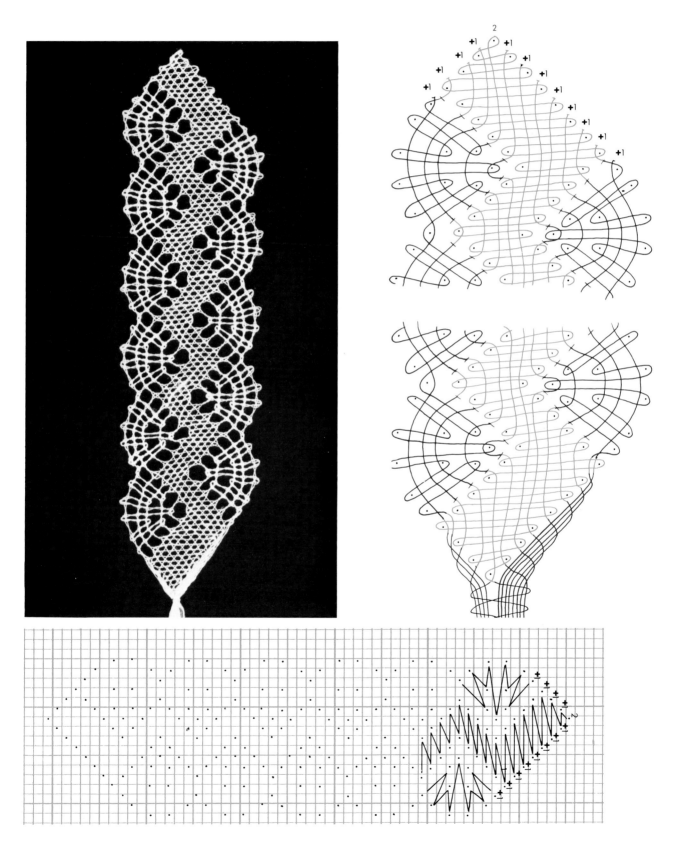

Bookmark–3
16 pairs + 1 pair gimps

Ground–WS, **A**
Motif–CS diamond, **A**
Spider–Small, **A** and with hole, **C1**
Gimp–Passing 1G, **A** and 2G together, **E**
Sewing edge–WS, **A**
Start–With 8 pair, **C**
Ending–With pairs inside (*exchanging worker with outside pair*), **B**

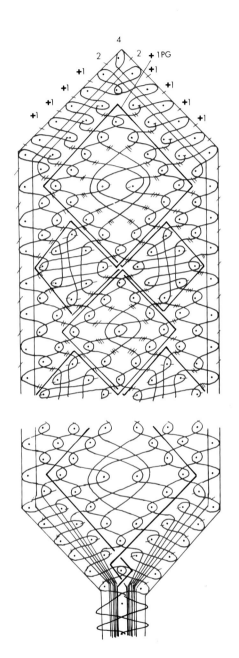

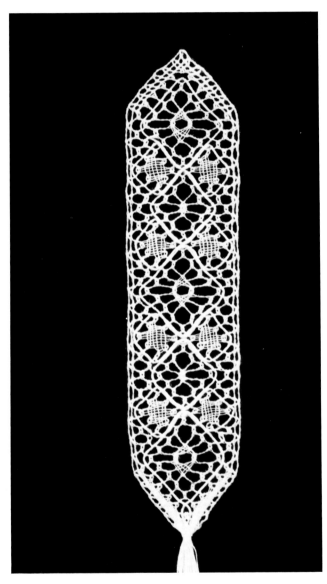

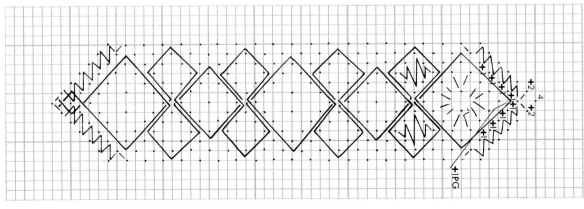

Bookmark–4
18 pairs + 2 pairs gimps

Ground–WS, **A**
Motif–Clover in CS
Spider–Small, **A**
Gimp–Passing 1G, **A** and 2G together, **E**
Sewing edge–WS, **A1**
Start–WS with 2 pairs, + adding, **B**
Ending–With pairs inside sewing edge
   (*exchanging worker with inside pairs*), **C**

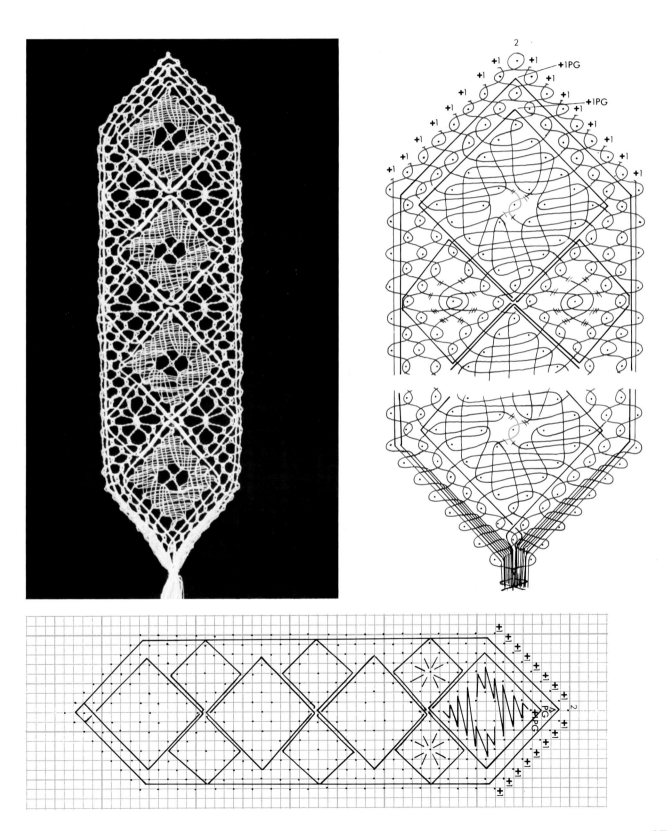

Bookmark–5
21 pairs

Ground–Torchon, **B**
Motif–Diagonal Rosepoint, **D1** and **D2**
Spider–Small, **A**
Sewing edge–WS, **A**
Beginning–With 8 pair, **C**
Ending–With pairs inside sewing edge
    (*exchanging worker with outside pair*), **B**

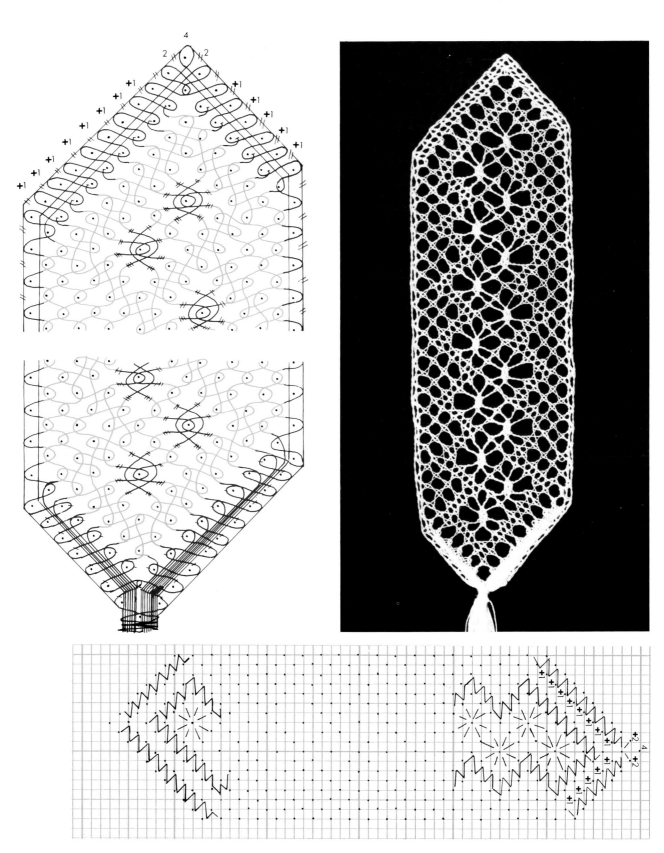

Bookmark–6
22 pairs

Ground–Simple Rosepoint, **A**
Motif–Diagonal Rosepoint, **D1** and **D2**
Spider–Small, **A**
Sewing edge–WS as Rosepoint, **A4**
Start–With 8 pair, **C**
Ending–With passives inside (*exchanging worker with outside pair*), **B**

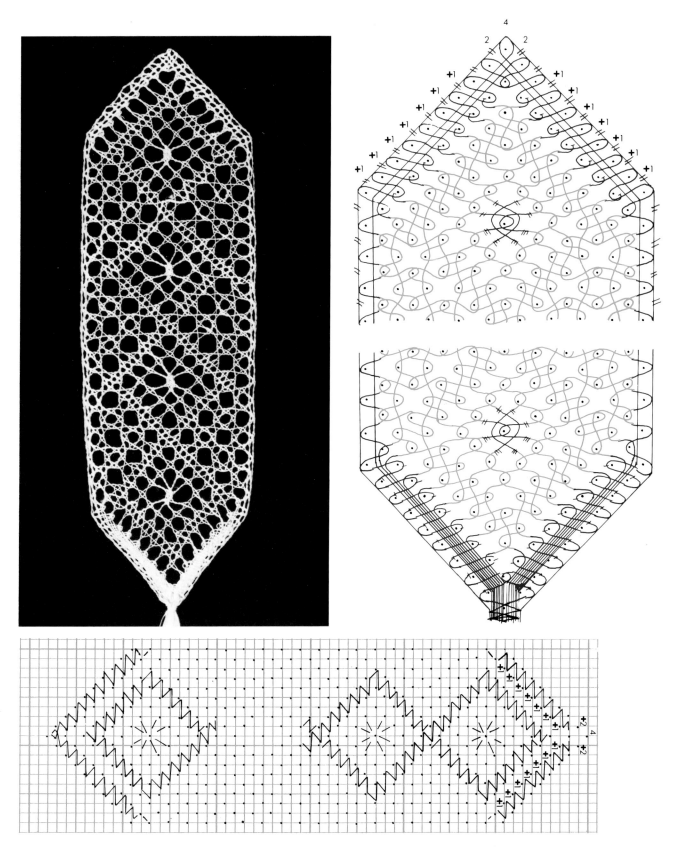

Bookmark–7
22 pairs
(*pricking p. 102*)

Ground–Dieppe, **C**
Motif–HS trail, **E2** (*creating window*)
Spider–Large, **B**
Sewing edge–WS, **A**
Start–With 8 pair, **C**
Ending–In WS eliminating pairs, **B**

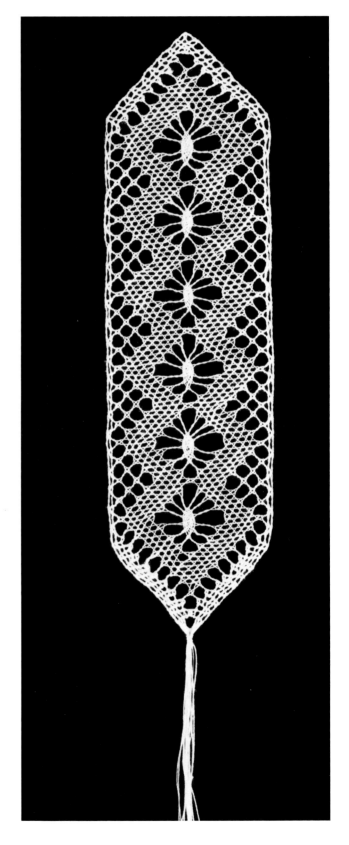

Bookmark–8
26 pairs
(*pricking p. 102*)

Motif–CS window, **F1**
Spider–Compound, **E**
Sewing edge–WS, **A**
Start–With 8 pair, **C**
Ending–With pairs inside SE eliminating
   pairs, **B**

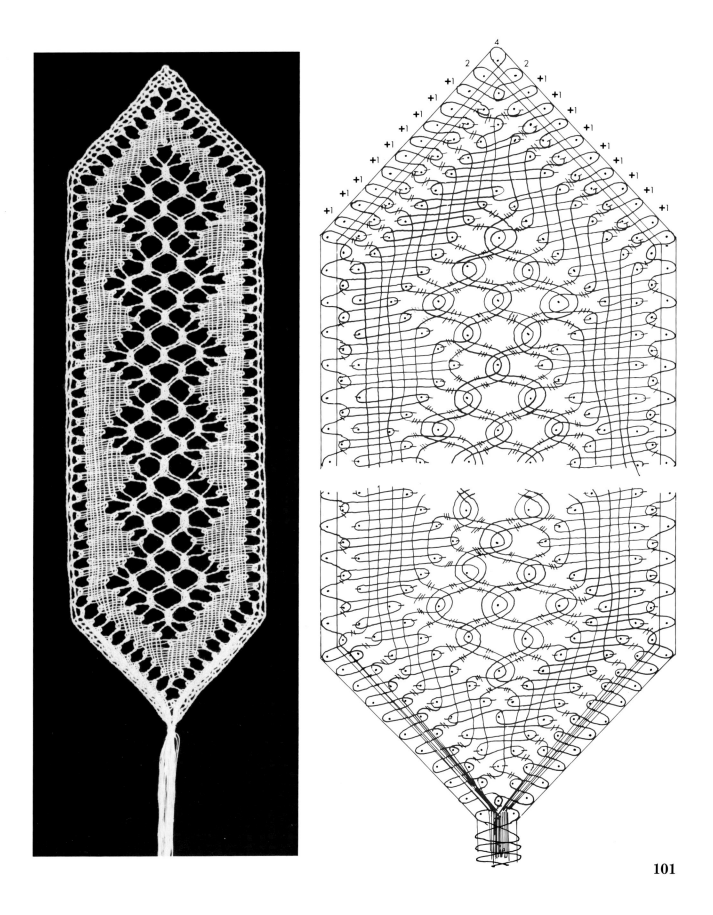

Bookmark–7
22 pairs
(*diagram and photo p. 100*)

Bookmark–8
26 pairs
(*diagram and photo p. 101*)

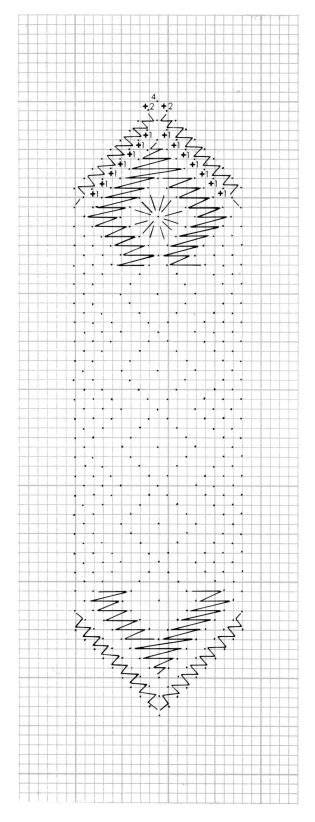

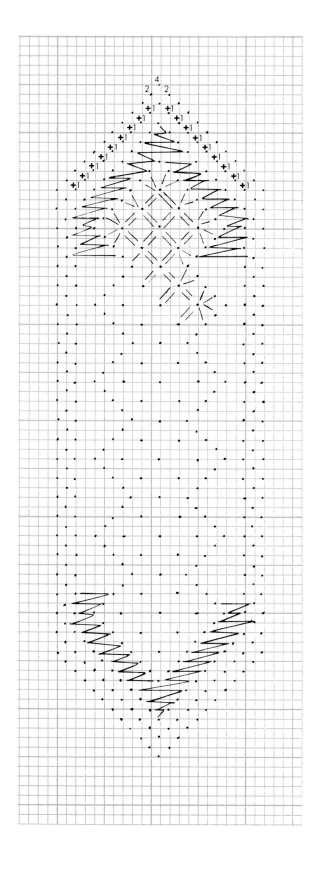

Bookmark–9
26 pairs
(diagram and photo p. 104)

Bookmark–10
28 pairs
(diagram and photo p. 105)

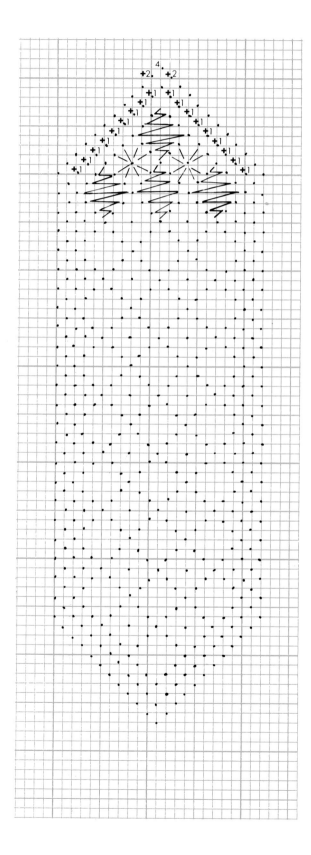

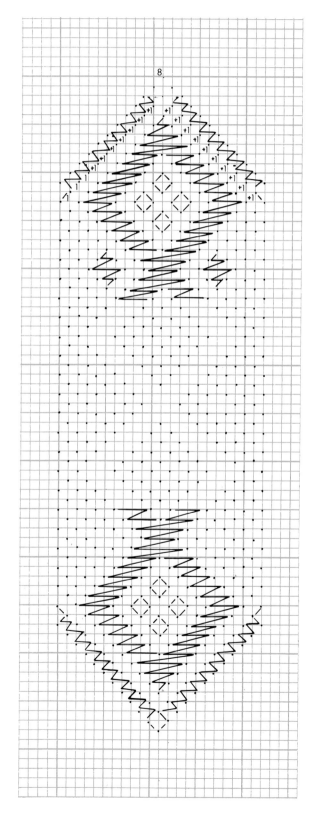

Bookmark–9
26 pairs
(*pricking p. 103*)

Ground–Dieppe, **C**
Motif–CS and HS diamond, **A1** and **A2**
Spider–Small, **A**
Sewing edge–WS, **A**
Start–With 8 pair, **C**
Ending–With pairs inside SE (*exchanging worker with outside pair*), **B**

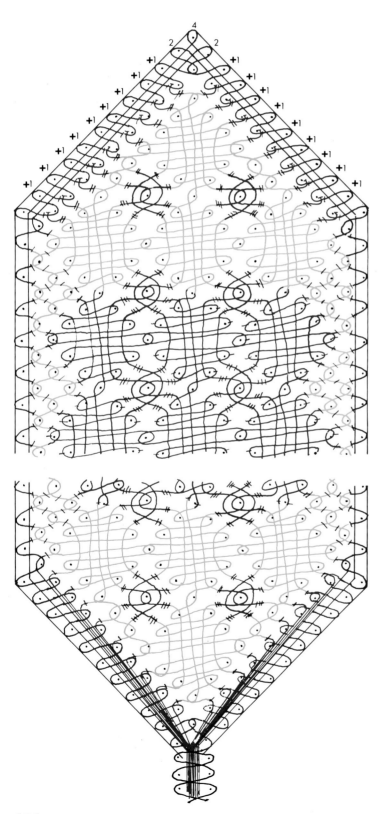

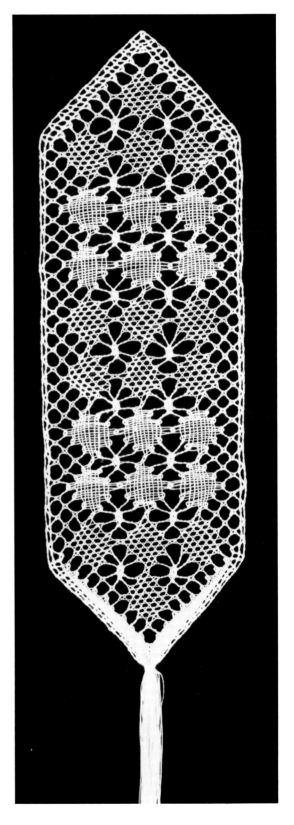

Bookmark–10

28 pairs
(*pricking p. 103*)

Ground–Dieppe, **C** and Simple Rosepoint, **A**
Motif–CS diamond, **A1** and CS window, **F1**
Sewing edge–WS with 2 CS passives, **B**
Start–With 8 pair in CS, **D**
Ending–With pairs inside SE eliminating
   pairs, **B**

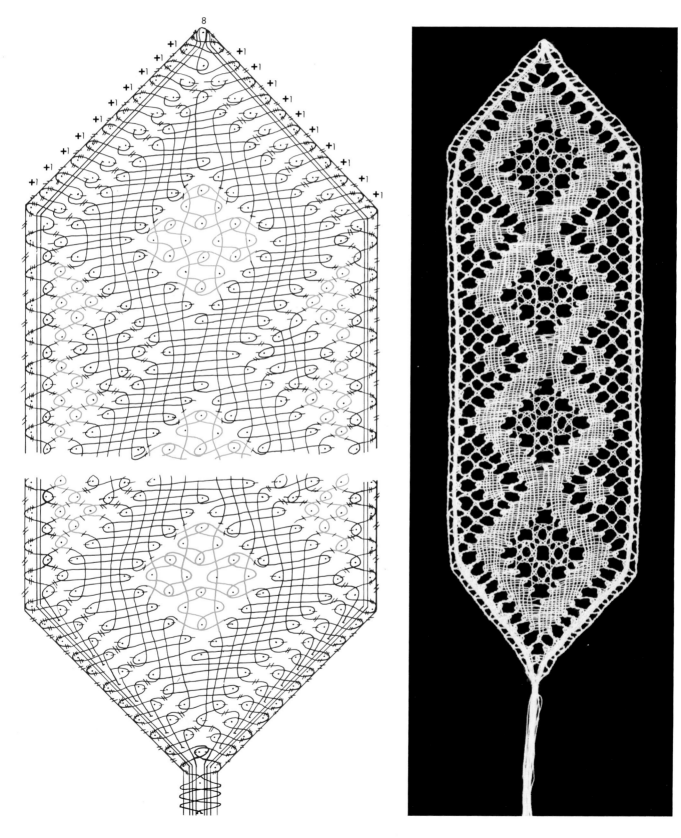

7.MEDALLIONS

Medallion–1
13 pairs

Ground–WS, **A**
Spider–Small, **A**
Fan–CS with WS on edge and twist, **B2**
Start–With 2 pairs in WS at outside edge,
    adding pairs to centre (*see* Medallion p. xv, **A**)
Ending–Sewings (*see* Techniques
    Sewing, p. xv)

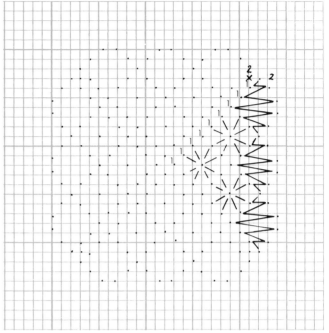

Medallion–2 (Doily)
14 pairs
(*photo p. 108 and diagram p. 109*)

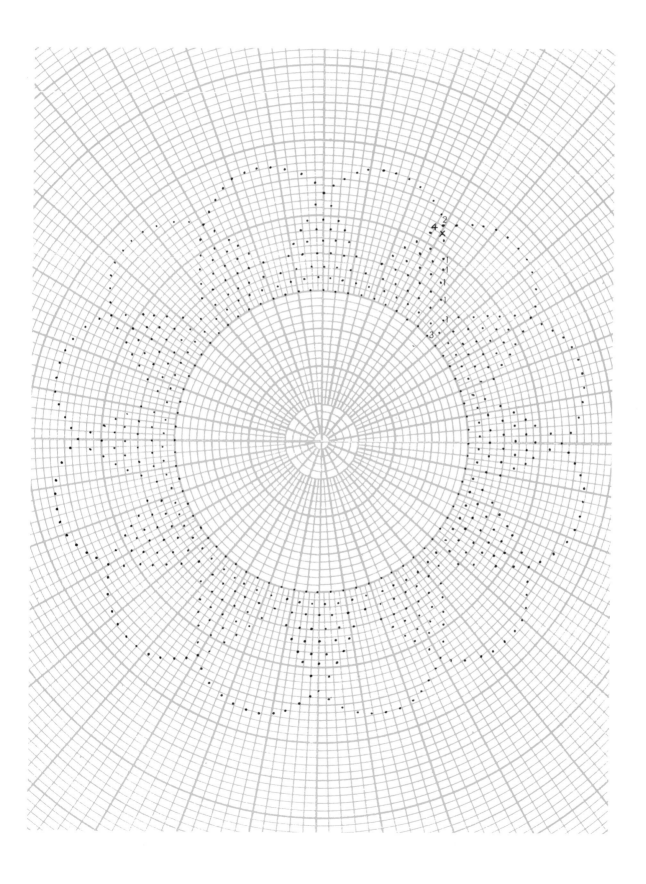

Medallion–2 (Doily)
13 pairs*
(*pricking p. 107 and diagram p. 109*)

*Diagram and pricking have extra pinholes in
ground requiring 14 pairs

Medallion–2 (Doily)
14 pairs
(*pricking p. 107 and photo p. 108*)

Ground–Torchon, **B**
Fan–CS with WS at edge and twist, **B1** and **B2**
Footing–WS, **A**
Start–With 2 pairs in WS at outer edge, adding pairs to centre (*see* Medallion, p. xv, **A**)
Ending–Sewings (*see* Techniques, *Sewing*, p. xv)

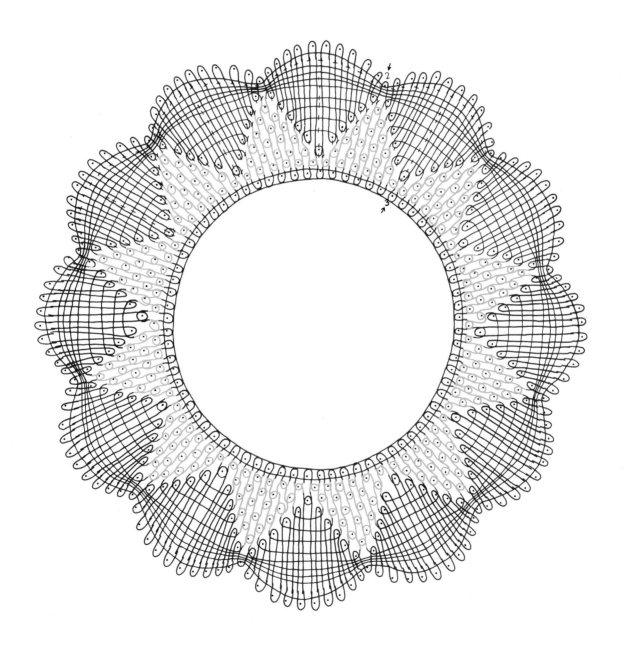

Medallion–3
17 pairs
(*diagram p. 111*)

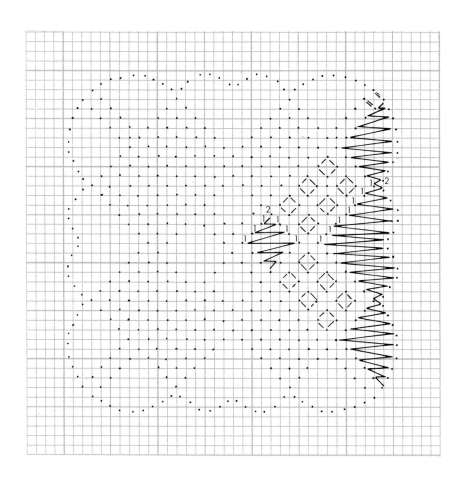

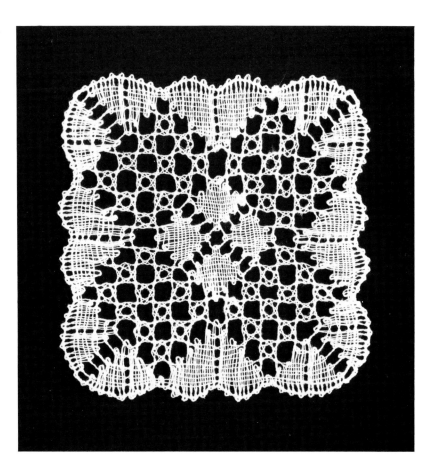

Medallion–3
17 pairs
(*pricking and photo p. 110*)

Ground–Rosepoint with WS corners, **B**
Motif–Cloth diamond, **A1**
Braid–Single on corners, **A**
Fan–CS with WS on edge and twist, **B2**
Start–With 2 pairs, in WS at outer edge, adding
pairs to centre – must complete CS diamond
before beginning Rosepoint (*see* Medallion,
p. xv, **A**)
Ending–Sewings (*see* Techniques,
Sewing, p. xv)

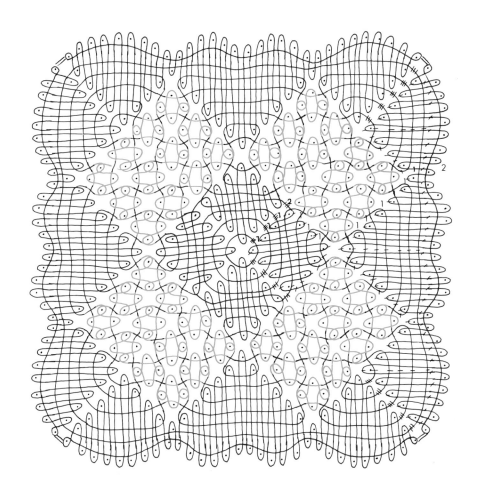

Medallion–4
19 pairs
(*diagram p. 113*)

Medallion–4
19 pairs
(*pricking and photo p. 112*)

Ground–WS, **A**
Motif–CS diamond, **A1** and Diagonal
 Rosepoint, **D1** and **D2**
Spider–Small, **A**
Fan–Trellis, **C**
Start–With 2 pairs in HS at the beginning of the
 Diagonal Rosepoint, adding pairs along the
 diagonal towards the centre and the outside
 edge, adding 3 pairs for fan (*see* Medallion,
 p. xv, **A**)
Ending–Sewings (*see* Techniques,
 Sewing, p. xv)

Medallion–5
21 pairs
(*diagram p. 115*)

114

Medallion–5
21 pairs
(*pricking and photo p. 114*)

Ground–WS, **A**
Motif–CS chevron/heart, **D1**
Spider–Large, **B**
Fan–Trellis with CS, **C2**
Start–With 2 pairs in WS at top of Spider Motif, adding pairs along the diagonal towards the centre and the outside edge, adding 3 pairs for fan (*see* Medallion, p. xv, **A**)
Ending–Sewings (*see* Techniques, *Sewing*, p. xv)

Medallion–6

24 pairs
(*diagram p. 117 and pricking p. 118*)

Medallion–6
24 pairs
(*photo p. 116 and pricking p. 118*)

Motif–CS trail and HS chevron, **E1** and **D2**
Spider–Small compound, **E**
Fan–Trellis and Trellis with CS, **C** and **C2**
Start–With 2 pairs in CS at the beginning of the
   CS trail, adding pairs along the diagonal
   towards the centre (leave the 2 pairs for spider
   to be worked at the finish), adding 2 pairs at
   edge for fan (*see* Medallion, p. xv, **A**)
Ending–Sewings (*see* Techniques,
   Sewing, p. xv)

Medallion–6

24 pairs
(*photo p. 116 and diagram p. 117*)

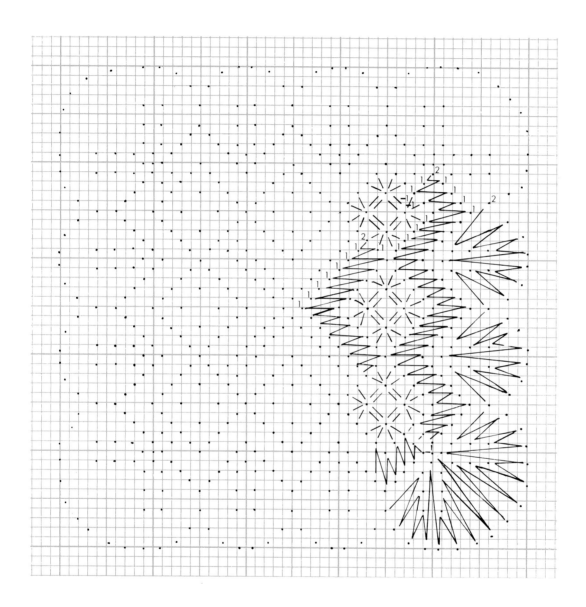

Medallion–7
29 pairs
(*photo p. 120 and diagram p. 121*)

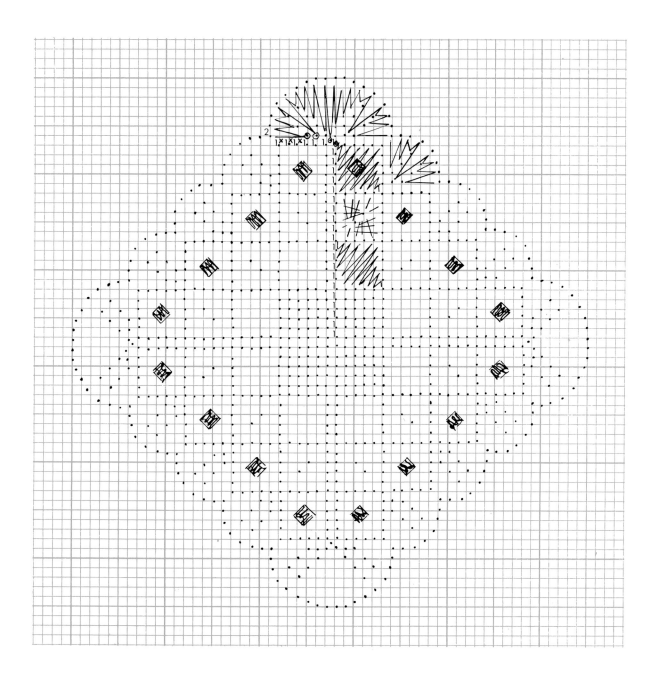

Medallion–7
29 pairs
(pricking p. 119 and diagram p. 121)

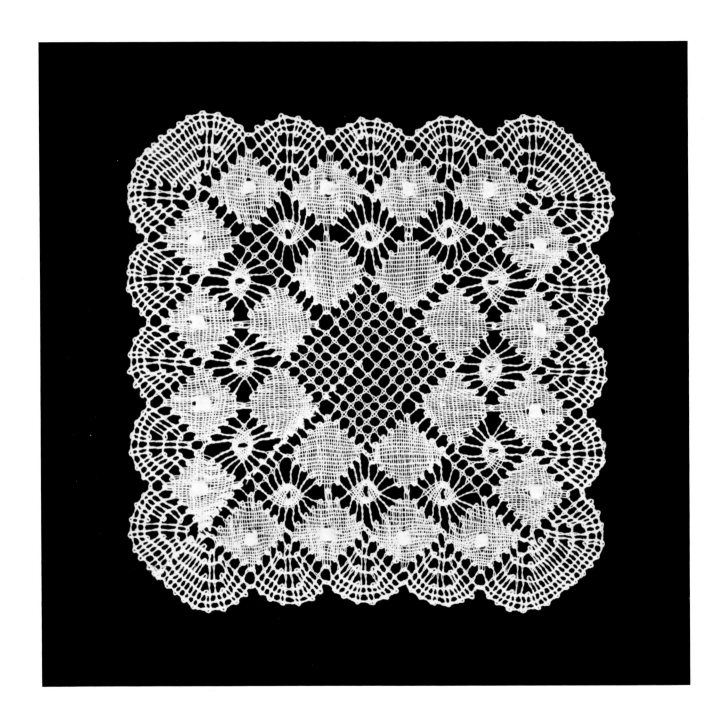

Medallion–7

29 pairs
(*pricking p. 119 and photo p. 120*)

Ground–Torchon, **B**
Motif–CS diamond, **A1** and CS diamond with
    raised tally (*see* Detail)
Spider–With hole, **C1**
Fan–Trellis, **C**
Start–With 2 pairs in WS at the beginning of
    the corner fan, adding pairs to complete fan,
    then adding pairs along the diagonal towards
    the centre (*see* Medallion, p.xv, **A**)
Ending–Sewings (*see* Techniques,
    Sewing, p. xv, **A**)

Detail
CS diamond with raised tally (*see* Tally p. 5, **A**)

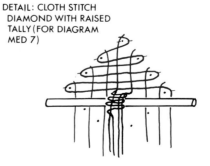

DETAIL: CLOTH STITCH
DIAMOND WITH RAISED
TALLY (FOR DIAGRAM
MED 7)

121

Medallion–8
36 pairs
(*diagram p. 123*)

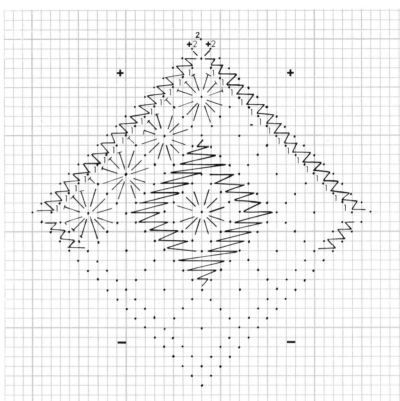

Medallion–8
36 pairs
(*pricking and photo p. 122*)

Stitch–WS, **A**
Motif–CS window, **F1**
Spider–Large, **B**
Sewing edge–WS with 2 WS passives, **A1**
Start–With 6 pairs, (*see* Techniques, *Starts*,
    p. xv, – Variation, **C** and Medallion, p. xv, **B**)
Ending–Eliminating pairs (*see* Medallion,
    p. xv, **B**)

Medallion–9
42 pairs
(*diagram p. 125*)

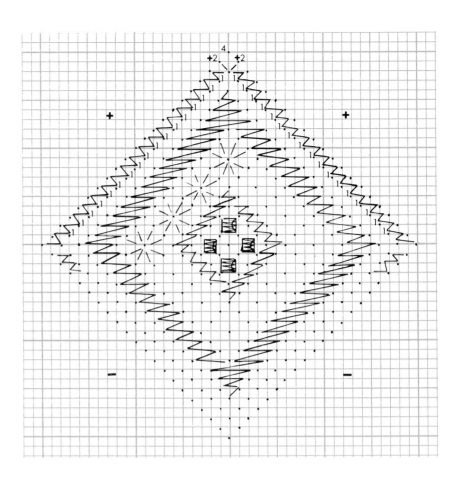

Medallion–9
42 pairs
(*pricking and photo p. 124*)

Ground–WS, **A**
Motif–CS window, **F1**
Spider–Small, **A**
Tally–4 with ground, **C** (*see* Detail, p. 5)
Sewing edge–WS with 2 WS passives, **A3**
Start–With 8 pairs, (*see* Medallion, p. xv, **B**)
Ending–Eliminating pairs (*see* Medallion,
 p. xv, **B**)

Medallion–10
44 pairs
(*diagram p. 127*)

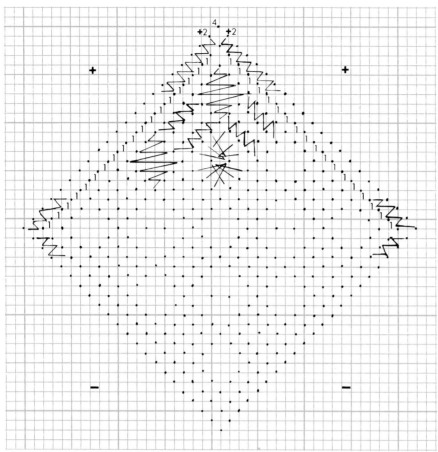

Medallion–10
44 pairs
(*pricking and photo p. 126*)

Motif–CS diamond, **A1** and Diagonal
  Rosepoint, **D1** and **D2**
Spider–Large with hole, **C1**
Sewing edge–WS with 2 WS passives, **A3**
Start–With 8 pairs (*see* Medallion, p. xv, **B**)
Ending–Eliminating pairs (*see* Medallion,
  p. xv, **B**)

BIBLIOGRAPHY

Books in English with techniques and patterns recommended for beginning to intermediate students:

Clare, Raie, *The Dryad Book of Bobbin Lace*, London, Dryad Press Ltd

Fisher, Jennifer, *Torchon Lace for Today*, London, Dryad Press Ltd

Groves, Edna, *A New Approach to Embroidered Net*, London, Dryad Press Ltd

Harris, Valerie, *The Lavendon Collection of Bobbin Lace Patterns*, London, Dryad Press Ltd

Hills, Ros, *Colour and Texture in Needlelace*, London, Dryad Press Ltd

Holmes, Doreen, *Flowers in Needlepoint Lace*, London, Dryad Press Ltd

Nottingham, Pamela, *Bobbin Lace Making*, London, B.T. Batsford Ltd

Nottingham, Pamela, *The Technique of Bobbin Lace*, London, B.T. Batsford Ltd

Nottingham, Pamela, *The Technique of Torchon Lace*, London, B.T. Batsford Ltd

Southard, Doris, *Bobbin Lacemaking*, USA, Chas. Scribner's Sons*

Stillwell, Alexandra, *Drafting Torchon Lace Patterns*, London, Dryad Press Ltd

Sutton, Edna, *Bruges Flower Lace*, London, Dryad Press Ltd

Withers, Jean, *Mounting and Using Lace*, London, Dryad Press Ltd

This book is used extensively in the USA as a beginner's first book – the largest controversy is the use of TC for half stitch (called half throw which distinguishes the stitch from CT) as in the French text, Les Dentelles Aux Fuseau. Encouragement should be given to beginning students to be aware of the existence of these differences between countries' methods. Once they are aware of this, they can readily use books regardless of origin.

Manuals, history, reference and identification material recommended:

Bullock, Alice-May, *Lace and Lacemaking*, London, B.T. Batsford Ltd

Cook, Bridget M. and Stott, Geraldine, *Book of Bobbin Lace Stitches*, London, B.T. Batsford and USA, Chas. T. Branford

Earnshaw, Pat, *A Dictionary of Lace*, Aylesbury, Shire Publications Ltd

Earnshaw, Pat, *Bobbin & Needle Laces: Identification and Care*, London, B.T. Batsford Ltd, and available through Robin and Russ Handweavers, USA

Earnshaw, Pat, *The Identification of Lace*, London, B.T. Batsford Ltd, and USA, Shire Publications Ltd

Maidment, Margaret, *Manual of Handmade Bobbin Lacework*. First published in 1931. Reprinted London, B.T. Batsford and available through Robin and Russ Handweavers, USA

More advanced Torchon books recommended (*some not available in English*):

Egger, Katharina, *Kloppeln*, Switzerland, Verlag Paul Haup Berne and Stuttgart, 1981

Egger, Katharina, *Neue Kloppelmuster*, Switzerland, Verlag Paul Haup Berne, 1984

Hardeman, Henk, *Torchonpatronen*, Westland, Schoten, Cantecleer bv, de Bilt, 1984, Tweede druk, 1985

Les Dentelles Aux Fuseau, (English abbreviated, translation by Mary McPeek), Thérèse de Dillmont Editions, Ltd., reprinted USA: Gale Research Co., 1974

Nissen, Karen Trend, *Knippling (1)* and *Knippling 2*, Borgen, 1984

Olson, Inga-Lisa, *Knypplerskan I & II, III*, Sweden, Forlag A/BE Homgvists EFTR, 1982-3

Zwaal-Lint, Tiny, *Bobbin Lace Patterns* (English translation by Pamela Nottingham), London, B.T. Batsford, 1984

For many years there were few books available, those that were were reprints of old editions or out-of-print copies difficult to find and expensive to obtain. Within the last five years there have been numerous books written and published offering a wide selection of books covering many areas of lace. These have become too numerous to detail here. This selection is restricted to those deemed most helpful to beginning and intermediate students.

SUPPLIERS

UNITED KINGDOM

BEDFORDSHIRE
A. Sells
49 Pedley Lane
Clifton
Shefford SG17 5QT

BERKSHIRE
Chrisken Bobbins
26 Cedar Drive
Kingsclere RG15 8TD

BUCKINGHAMSHIRE
J.S. Sear
Lacecraft Supplies
8 Hillview
Sherington MK16 9NJ

CAMBRIDGESHIRE
Josie and Jeff Harrison
Walnut Cottage
Winwick
Huntingdon PE17 5PP

Spangles
Carole Morris
Cashburn Lane
Burwell CB5 0ED

CHESHIRE
Lynn Turner
Church Meadow Crafts
7 Woodford Road
Winsford

DEVON
Honiton Lace Shop
44 High Street
Honiton EX14 8PJ

DORSET
Frank Herring & Sons
27 High West Street
Dorchester DT1 1UP

GLOUCESTERSHIRE
Chosen Crafts Centre
46 Winchcombe Street
Cheltenham GL52 2ND

KENT
D.J. Hornsby
25 Manwood Avenue
Canterbury CT1 7AH

Frances Iles
73 High Street
Rochester ME1 1LX

MERSEYSIDE
Hayes & Finch
Head Office & Factory
Hanson Road
Aintree
Liverpool L9 9BP

MIDDLESEX
Redburn Crafts
Squires Garden Centre
Halliford Road
Upper Halliford
Shepperton TW17 8RU

NORFOLK
Alby Lace Museum
Cromer Road
Alby
Norwich NR11 7QE

NORTH YORKSHIRE
Just Lace
14 Ashwood Gardens
Gildersome
Leeds LS27

Stitchery
6 Finkle Street
Richmond DL10 46A

NORTHANTS
Anna's Lace Chest
1 Gorse Close
White Hills
Northamptonshire
NN2 8ED

SOUTH YORKSHIRE
D.H. Shaw
47 Lamor Crescent
Thrushcroft
Rotherham S66 9QD

SURREY
Needle and Thread
80 High Street
Horsell
Woking GU21 4SZ

Needlestyle
5 The Woolmead
Farnham GU9 7TX

SUSSEX
Southern Handicrafts
20 Kensington Gardens
Brighton BN1 4AC

WARWICKSHIRE
Christine & David Springett
21 Hillmorton Road
Rugby CV22 5DF

WEST MIDLANDS
The Needlewoman
21 Needles Alley
off New Street
Birmingham B2 5AE

Stitches
Dovehouse Shopping Parade
Warwick Road
Olton, Solihull

WEST YORKSHIRE
Sebalace
Waterloo Mills
Howden Road
Silsden BD20 0HA

SCOTLAND
Christine Riley
53 Barclay Street
Stonehaven
Kincardineshire

Peter & Beverley Scarlett
Strupak, Hill Head
Cold Wells, Ellon
Grampian

WALES
Bryncraft Bobbins
B.J. Phillips
Pantglas, Cellan
Lampeter
Dyfed SA48 8JD

Hilkar Lace Suppliers
33 Mysydd Road
Landore
Swansea

AUSTRALIA
Dentelles Lace Supplies
c/o Betty Franks
39 Lang Terrace
Northgate 4013
Brisbane
Queensland

Lace Craft
Valerie Dunsmore
3 Barton Drive
Mount Eliza
Victoria 3930

Lace Inspirations
Joanne Pope
16 Robertson Road
Leopold
Victoria 3224

J.O. O'Brien
61 Bligh Avenue
Camden
NSW 2570

NEW ZEALAND
Peter McLeavey
P.O. Box 69.007
Auckland 8

USA
Arbor House
22 Arbor Lane
Roslyn Heights
NY 11577

Baltazor Inc
3262 Severn Avenue
Metairie
LA 7002

Beggars' Lace
P.O. Box 481223
Denver
Colo 80248

Berga Ullman Inc.
P.O. Box 918
North Adams
MA 01247

Happy Hands
3007 S.W. Marshall
Pendleton
Oreg 97180

International Old Lacers
P.O. Box 1029
Westminster
Colo 80030

The Lacemaker
176 Sunset Avenue South
Edmonds
WA 98020

Lacis
3163 Adeline Street
Berkeley
CA 94703

Robin's Bobbins
RT1 Box 1736
Mineral Bluff
GA 30559-9736

Robin and Russ
Handweavers
533 North Adams Street
McMinnville
Oreg 97128

The Unique And Art Lace
  Cleaners
5926 Delman Boulevard
St Louis
MO 63112

Van Sciver Bobbin Lace
130 Cascadilla Park
Ithaca
NY 14850

INDEX